ALONE IN A ROOM

SECRETS OF SUCCESSFUL SCREENWRITERS

JOHN SCOTT LEWINSKI

Published by Michael Wiese Productions
11288 Ventura Blvd, Suite 621
Studio City CA 91604
Tel. (818) 379-8799
Fax (818) 986-3408
mw@mwp.com
www.mwp.com

Cover Design: Patrick Murdoch
Layout: Gina Mansfield
Editor: Paul Norlen
Original Illustrations: Richard Krzmenien, www.TheWriterAtWork.com

Printed by McNaughton & Gunn, Inc., Saline, Michigan
Manufactured in the United States of America

Library of Congress Cataloging-in-Publication Data

Lewinski, John Scott.
  Alone in a room : secrets of successful screenwriters / John Scott Lewinski.
      p. cm.
  Includes bibliographical references.
  ISBN 0-941188-93-0
  1. Motion picture authorship. I. Title.
  PN1996.L437 2004
    808.2'3--dc22
                              2004005512

"John Scott Lewinski provides an entertaining, informative, yet realistic take on the entertainment industry. His book offers a rare view of Hollywood's inner-workings from a writer's perspective that's educational and never cynical or bitter."

— J. C. Spink, Producer
(*The Ring, The Butterfly Effect*)

"Of all the books on screenwriting, here is the one that lets you get close to the experience at the most intimate level, to learn from those that do, and to realize that you're not alone. Writing a great screenplay is a challenge for everyone who attempts it, even those that have done it many times and cashed the paycheck. And, as this book attests, it is always worth doing."

— Meg LeFauve, Producer
(*The Dangerous Lives of Altar Boys, The Baby Dance*)

"Facing the blank page is a daunting task and the writers interviewed in Lewinski's book demonstrate how they tackle their jobs with creativity, energy, and most of all with persistence. A valuable addition to any writer's bookshelf — but don't keep it there. Read it and learn."

— Michael Halperin, Screenwriter, Author
(*Writing Great Characters* and *Writing the Second Act*)

"John Scott Lewinski is a dedicated student of writing and a student of the entertainment industry. He managed to get professionals to say on the record what every aspiring screenwriter needs to know. His book is a must for every writer hoping to prepare for a career in the business."

— Garfield Reeves-Stevens
Producer, Screenwriter, Author

"With a straight-shooting and take no prisoners approach to the craft and business of screenwriting, John Scott Lewinski offers writers a realistic look at what it takes to be a successful screenwriter, including advice from working writers and Lewinski's own experiences. He clearly knows what he's talking about, and shares his wisdom with razor-sharp style."

— Amy Brozio-Andrews, Managing Editor
AbsoluteWrite.com

"Finally, here's a screenwriting interview book that answers the questions writers-in-waiting (not film historians and other already-satisfied insiders) want to know. And that's because author Lewinski is a wonderful screenwriter himself, as well as a student of the craft and the crafter. Within these pages are enough word byte highlights to influence your work as a progressing script creator for years to come."

— Pam Pierce
Author and Executive Director of *CineStory*

"John Scott Lewinski has been a senior writer for *Scr(i)pt Magazine* for almost a decade. He has covered all aspects of the industry from writing to selling, and is truly a journalist on the inside of the business. His articles are always full of excellent advice and hard truths — every screenwriter should read them."

— Shelly Mellot
Editor in Chief, *Scr(i)pt Magazine*

"Knowledge is power, and we all know that when it comes to the movie business, power is everything. *Alone in a Room* is like a flashlight that you, the writer, can shine on the shadowy corners of a game based upon the power of creativity to sell tickets and make a lot of people rich and famous. By learning the rules and realities of the game, you can not only partake in all the fun and excitement... but maybe even score big and win. At the very least you'll have a great time playing."

— Marie Jones
Book Reviewer, *AbsoluteWrite.com*

"As a journalist and screenwriter, John Scott Lewinski brings industry savvy to his work. He's a student of the industry, and he brings that enthusiasm to this book."

— Beth Bohn, Agent, APA

table of contents

dedication

I had so many teachers over the years, and I am grateful to all of them for their selfless effort and vital impact on my life. Judith and Garfield Reeves-Stevens keep me in mind of all of them. Kind, helpful, and eager to share their combined experience and wisdom, they never fail to amaze me with their generosity. They are simply far too kind to be so successful in Hollywood.

acknowledgements

I would like to thank Dr. Michael Halperin for his mentoring and for making introductions; Michael Wiese, Ken Lee and everyone at Michael Wiese Productions for their patience and input; J.C. Spink and everyone at Benderspink for opening their doors to me; Peter Woodke, Esq. for his friendship and advice; Meg LeFauve for pointing me in the right direction; Beth Bohn at APA for offering assistance; Shelly Mellot and everyone at Scr(i)pt Magazine for a little promo; Richard Krzemien, for making sure my book came with pictures; and, of course, all of the generous and insightful professionals who agreed to participate and granted me interviews for this book.

introduction

"Paint the Windows Black"

I like the movie and TV business — and, I don't mean merely writing for it. I like the bottom-line, cutthroat, perform or perish nature of the industry. It's best to get that out now so you know what you're getting into before you start flipping pages. A lot of the material here is harsh — potentially frightening or professionally offensive. At first glance, you might think this is some sort of sardonic exposé of writing for the entertainment business. Actually, William Goldman already wrote that book perfectly well — three or four times by now. I include the tough side of this profession because it fascinates me. I love the pure Darwinism of Hollywood. You must have talent, ambition, determination, confidence, a little luck, and, maybe, a touch of insanity to stick with this line of work. And, if you don't have all of those ingredients, not only won't you succeed — Hollywood will scrape you off its boot.

So many writers bemoan those aspects of the game, complaining that "good stories" and talented writers are consistently ignored by an establishment that concentrates too much on marketing and ticket sales. After I ask if they want cheese with their whine, I remind them that they can spend their energy complaining about Hollywood and its practices, or they can start learning them and figuring out how to play along to their greater benefit. Somebody out there is writing the movies being bought and made. I believe the difference between those doing the work and those longing for the jobs is the ability to accept the realities of the business and be able to perform effectively within those realities.

My first job out of film school in the mid-1990s was working for a video game company in Las Vegas. The CD-ROM games the company made combined cinematic cut scenes with actual game play, and it was my job to write them. This manufacturer employed producers, art designers, actors, and directors to create the cinematic scenes, and many of them were imported from Hollywood. However, they were all cast-offs of the studios. Most of the art designers washed out of Hollywood gigs. The director took his shot at the big time and failed. There was a lot of collective bitterness over Hollywood practices — and a lot of hope that the interactive entertainment genre would offer them the success that mainstream show business denied them.

Since the company made games, and not movies, they naturally defended their evolving interactive story format as the future of storytelling. Some even believed that the days of traditional movies were coming to an end. Strangely enough, all these "anti-movie" folks also decorated their offices with film memorabilia and filled their work with cinematic allusions. In the end, they were howlingly, spectacularly wrong about the imminent demise of movies, and their company was later bought out by a bigger and more successful company. However, through all of this, they complained about how movies were conceived, written, produced, directed, marketed, et cetera. I wondered why they ever tried to get into the movie business if they hated the creative process and the resulting products so much. They reminded me of a running back who complains about football because he gets tackled. I'd ask them, if they didn't like the rules of the game, why did they step off of the sidelines?

There is no room in Hollywood or the creative work driving it for bitterness. The movie business doesn't owe you a thing. It doesn't owe the American public or our collective cultural psyche anything either.

The town provides entertainment and makes money selling it. If you can understand that and come to terms with it, you will be more than welcome to try and feed that entertainment profiteering machine with stories that grew in your imagination. That's the fun part. So, what you give up on the front end in "artistic integrity," you can pick up on the back end in that proverbial land of "make-believe."

Hollywood does not exist to give an outlet to your voice or to make high art with every single production. Along the way, outstanding artistic achievements can result from the combined efforts of countless creative professionals all reaching for excellence. However, as you well know, such films are the exception and not the norm. More often, that studio flick you're watching over your silo of popcorn and your tankard of sugar water is intended purely for your escapist pleasure. If this fact bothers you, you're not a movie lover. Again, the entertainment business is on this planet to entertain and (like every other business in the world) make money. The sooner you understand and accept all of that, the sooner you can get down to writing material that'll get in the door with a serious opportunity at making you some money as a writer.

Now, obviously, some films absolutely achieve the lofty goals of revolutionary quality. We all have our favorite classics — be they heart-wrenching dramas dripping with pathos or blockbusters that redefined the boundaries of the genre. If you became a writer to wrought your agony upon the world, to share you personal therapy with the masses, or to generate the cinematic reincarnations of *Catcher in the Rye* or *The Sun Also Rises* with every typed word, get out of Dodge. If you want to control every aspect of a story by your strict artistic vision, write stage plays. If you want to say precisely what your heart wants you to say without compromise, write poetry. Just don't expect anybody to read it.

As you'll learn in the pages to follow, writing for the entertainment industry is a collaborative medium in which the writer is only one part of the process — hardly in control of the finished product. He or she should give his or her absolute best effort to shape the words on the script page as skillfully as possible to contribute a maximum vision to the final product. But, after that, it's going to development executives, producers, directors, actors, and editors. As one of the professionals you'll meet later in this book explained to me, making a movie is like running a relay race with an Olympic team. The writer is the first sprinter out of the gate — carrying that baton (the story) as if it was the most precious commodity on the planet because, to the writer, it truly is. However, as the writer rounds the first turn and completes his or her leg of the relay race, it comes time to give up the baton and let the next speedster run with it. You must be prepared for that moment in which you let go of the story and watch the next member of the team run with it. You'll meet up with them again at the finish line and hopefully enjoy the fruits of victory together.

So, I set out to write a book that works to empower you as that first, brave racer. You are out there running your heart out with your scripts, and you want to give yourself (and anyone who works on your stories in the future) the best shot at winning the creative race. Perhaps you'll want to consider this book part of your training — one of the many wind sprints you must run to get yourself in shape. Just as the athlete must endure pain and disillusionment along the road to victory, you have to face some hard truths about the industry that you might not like to hear. But, by arming yourself with such information, you're better equipped to hurdle those obstacles. (Okay, I'll lay off the sports analogies for a little while.)

In my experience, there are generally two kinds of screenwriting books. The first is strictly how-to — dealing mainly with the details of how to write scripts for TV and film. Obviously, we need books like this. Not everyone can get into or afford film school, and there aren't writing classes in every town across America.

However, the second breed of book deals with making it in the industry. I find some of these tomes to be a little too "kumbaya" and "up with people." Their collective tone can seem overly simplistic and blindingly encouraging — sort of "Come to the picnic and enjoy a frou-frou marshmallow land of wonderful dreams. Golly gee... You can do it." And the truth more often is, if you don't know the business you're getting into, you can't do it. You'll be chewed up and spat out quicker than the chewing tobacco between a pitcher's cheek and gum. (Oops. Sorry. I did promise about the sports analogies, didn't I?) So, while I don't want to discourage anyone hoping to write for Hollywood, I do want to prepare you for some of the rougher sides of the business so you'll be more apt to avoid the pitfalls.

Through my observations and the input of countless interviewed professionals, this book outlines the realities of writing for Hollywood. I'm not arrogant or foolish enough to think that I have all of the answers or to spout off for 200+ pages on all of my hard-won wisdom. (Actually, I really am arrogant enough, but I'm not foolish enough to try and do all of that typing from scratch.) So, as I said, I include several interviews with working professionals in various roles and in various stages of their careers. More importantly, I managed to get many of them to say on the record what they never dared to say to any other publication or media outlet. Some clearly dismissed the limits of Hollywood PC and "let 'er rip" on the tough realities of showbiz. You get the benefit of the truth on these pages and can walk into this industry with your eyes wide open.

The idea is to detail what essential truths the professionals here learned from their humble beginnings up until their eventual successes so you have a better idea of what to expect — detailing how you need to "gird your loins" for battle, so to speak. (I can't believe I managed to work the word "loins" into this.) Many of those lessons will deal with how you deal with criticism, handle rejection, market yourself and your work, et cetera. But many more will confront the tricks and secrets of professional Hollywood writing — illustrating how writers working at the highest levels knuckle down and get the work done.

When it's just you, "alone in a room," and there's no one else to turn to for help, you must perform — knowing you're a cog in a huge movie/TV development wheel. So, in the end, this book deals with what you need to know when you're considering what to write, developing your plan for writing it, writing the script itself, and presenting that work that you really think could make your way in this business. What do you have to keep in mind when you're on deadline and, if you miss the zero hour, you'll literally never work in this business again? When it comes time to paint the windows black, lock yourself in, and get the work done, what are the best professional practices to keep in mind?

I assume I'm going to upset a lot of writers with this book. They might consider my comments to be excessively negative and defeatist. However, I include nothing here that I have not personally observed. And the interviews I include are provided by working human beings that are already getting paid to do what you want to do. They have no reason to lie, and neither do I. We're describing the reality of the entertainment business and letting you decide if you're up to pursuing a livelihood in it.

So, we're about to step into the battle — to look the hard work and doubt square in the eye and decide if you're a warrior. You will either take a deep breath and accept the difficulties en route to your success, or you will decide it's too hard, too unfair and too uncertain. If you choose the latter path, go back to the farm. You're safer there where life is easier, quieter, safer... and boring. But if you really are a writer at heart who bangs out stories not because you want to, but because you have to, you are a soldier of words. You are a man or woman of courage, passion, and character. You belong in this business. You are needed in this business. And I hope once you see it for what it is, you'll be willing to hack your way through your enemies and find your path to a successful writing career. (Yes, I've foregone sports analogies for war allusions.) Which do you prefer?

section one

The Solitary Scribe

Dig deep to find your best work.

chapter one

One Man Band:
Daily Professionalism for the Lonely Screenwriter

I want to get this magnum opus off and running with a bang, so strap yourselves in, boys and girls. There's a great deal of eye-opening admissions en route. Some of this material will encourage you. Some will frighten you. And the rest will anger you. I was warned by a few industry folks here and there that too much of the harsh, white light of Hollywood truth and my book might do little else except drive aspiring writers out of the business. I say that if it's that easy to scare you off, I'm doing you a favor. You'd have been scraped off of somebody's boot out here eventually. Rather than run for the woods in indignant disbelief, take what's said here and arm yourself.

We begin with you, the individual screenwriter — taking up arms against a sea of producers, agents, managers, and development folk. You are a man or woman looking to make a living as a writer and to see stories forged largely in your own imagination reach a mass audience. You don't have a writing partner. You don't have a staff of editors and analysts. You may or may not be a member of a writer's group. You might have an agent or manager. You probably don't yet have enough income derived solely from your written work to support you full-time as a writer.

However, you better have a genuine love of stories (in movies, on TV, or in books). And you must enjoy the simple, serene, intimate process of sitting before a keyboard, typewriter, or pad and pen and creating written works. If you don't have that, why are you here? There are easier ways to make a living. If you do indeed possess the essentials, congratulations... You have a book named after you. You are the human being "alone in a room," and you find yourself in one of the most competitive businesses — and certainly the most competitive artistic venture — in the world. If you have the desire to stick to it in the face of that struggle, you should be proud of yourself.

Step One — Type.

Now, how do you get the work done? Obviously, there are entire libraries written on that problem, but the title of this book would seem to indicate that I have some insight into the struggles of the solitary scribe (and some minor ability for alliteration). I've interviewed hundreds of writers in my life — both officially and casually over mochas, lattes, et cetera. The best of those interviews grace these very pages, and most of those writers gladly include their tips on the basics (and secret tips) for getting the work done when the pressure's on and you must produce.

For now, I can list some basic similarities in their professional practices. Not all of these procedures will work for you now. I'm assuming most of the readers of this book are aspiring to make their living by writing. However, they may not be in that position. You probably have to set a couple of hours here and there to get your work done. Maybe you steal away in the morning before work or at night before hitting the rack. No matter what you have to do currently, you are looking forward to full-time writing. Here's a preview of your life to come.

Most professional Hollywood TV and film writers tend to keep some semblance of banker's hours. In most cities, that means 9 to 5. But who are we kidding? In Hollywood, banker's hours are more like 10:30 until the nightmarish traffic ends on the 405 or the 101. Some work in an office — sometimes on studio lots because their contract for whatever movie they're working on called for office space near the production. TV writers on sitcoms or one-hour drama shows almost always have office space because they need to be close by for last minute production rewrites — or they need to bounce ideas off of other staff writers.

More writers work from home, venturing forth for meetings and the safe haven of Starbucks. In that potentially lonely isolation, every writer finds his or her own procedures — some leaning toward the extreme. A screenwriter in Los Angeles (who shall remain nameless to make this book seem more dramatic and mysterious) works out of his home, as many writers do. While people in the nine to five, office-bound world believe the home office to be Shangri La, the concept is actually fraught with danger for a scribe. With writer's block lurking around the corner of every page, and distractions like the kitchen, cable TV, or video games only serving to encourage procrastination, it's all too easy to avoid work in your home's work space. Our screenwriter in question discovered a novel way around the home office's seductive traps. Every morning, he wakes up at 8 a.m., showers, dresses in business casual, and packs his briefcase. After kissing his wife "good bye," he heads out into the world — only to walk around the block and end up back at his front door. He walks back inside (without speaking to his wife), sits at his desk, and works until lunch. When it's time to eat, he grabs something out before settling back at his keyboard until 5 p.m. Then, and only then, he shuts down the word processor for the day, packs up, and walks around the block — arriving "home" again for dinner.

It may seem silly or unnecessary — even obsessive. But that ritual helps this writer get the work done and feed his family. Professional writers throughout various media and disciplines all have their own unique practices to make sitting "alone in a room" seem more like a traditional, workable job. These habits range from the fascinating to the inspirational to the hilarious. And we'll cover more of them as we move from comedy writers to writing staffs to writing teams, et cetera.

Even though you might do your writing work "alone in a room," you'll find that much of the material in this chapter and throughout the book discusses aspects of the writing business that take place when you are not alone — such as pitching or taking notes. However, it's vital to understand that you prepare for these activities when you are indeed alone and mentally considering your next move — be it creative, marketing-based, or some element of networking. You are a coach or a general, and you are also your army. You need to prepare yourself with sound professional practices whether you are writing, pitching, editing, et cetera.

So, What Do I Write?

The first stage in this Hollywood writer's process must be deciding what to write. Before you can even scribble down a working title or word one of a treatment or outline, you should carefully consider what story you're going to tell. It takes months to write a screenplay from log line through first draft to final draft, and you only get so many months in a year — and in your life, for that matter. Shouldn't you carefully consider what you're going to spend that portion of your life writing? I'm not suggesting you agonize over writing a comedy, drama, sci-fi adventure, or musical. I'm saying you should make certain it's a story that will sell (unless you're writing as a mere hobby... but, I think you want to make a little scratch at this game).

Here's the first major point where this pile of wood pulp in your paws will divert from the majority of screenwriting books out there. Most of the other writing books out there will tell you to "Write your passion" or "Find your voice." In most cases, you could translate that to mean "Starve to death" or "Take up professional gardening."

When you write a script, you are feeding the beast — fueling the entertainment industry monster that needs product. That industry pays you well for that product. Why wouldn't you want to supply what the industry wants? If you want to write for the film and television industry, you need to consider every idea you write in terms of marketability. You may not like that, but I guarantee you the people reading your scripts think that way. And they decide whether or not your script sells.

What makes a script marketable? We'll examine that throughout these pages. But even if you choose to develop your high-concept ideas, where do those concepts come from within your imagination? It's not just the art house story ideas that require creativity. Even the next summer blockbuster needs that initial spark of inspiration. The problem is, there is only one question about my writing I never answer: "Where do you get your inspiration?" Lack of forethought on my part — bringing up this topic? No. I think it's important to explain why I never discuss where, how, or why my ideas and motivation arise. I don't know, and I don't want to know. I don't want to figure out how I come up with my concepts. I don't want to analyze where creativity begins, ends, or why it exists in the first place. I believe that the second I delve too deep into those kind of answers — the moment I interfere with that nameless creative alchemy that gives rise to story ideas, characters, themes, or the passion to develop them — then the ideas won't come to me as easily anymore.

I believe that ideas and creative motivation arise from that nameless soup of intellect, emotion, psychology, personal history, and (perhaps most importantly) movie marketing savvy that cannot be dissected, studied, recreated, or bottled. So, when an idea comes to me (especially those concepts that seem unique and not inspired by an already existing story or genre — but that still fit the Hollywood high concept model), I take almost a third-person approach. I sit back and watch while the story unfolds before me as if someone else is telling it. I'm as surprised as my future readers are when a story comes together in my head, and I like a job that keeps surprising me. Why would I want to mess with it?

Well, a writer who messed with just about every possible question — be it related to inspiration, creativity, execution, revision or business — is the highly successful and influential screenwriter, David Goyer. There are plenty of interviews in this book. And we are definitely starting out with a bang.

David Goyer

A native of Ann Arbor, MI, David Goyer graduated from USC School of Cinema-Television. A popular comic book writer with partner Geoffrey Johns, Goyer is most famous for writing super hero stories, including *Batman 5*, the *Blade* series, *Dark City* and *Crow: City of Angels*.

While working on *Blade: Trinity* in Vancouver (and while writing *Batman 5* at the same time, mind you), Goyer agreed to offer his time and assorted advice to anyone looking to break into the entertainment industry as a screenwriter. In fact, during the brief interview, Goyer seemed very eager to get in as many pointers as he could — almost as if he felt the need to get some essential secrets out to you while knowing he didn't have that much time available. He was definitely very eager, honest, and helpful.

"First of all, be careful who you give your script to out there," Goyer said. "Don't trust anyone because there are a lot of liars in this business. A fairly well-known producer said I gave him a verbal option on something — which was untrue and totally illegal. And, it almost prevented me making my first sale if we hadn't bought him out. The threat of that sort of thing is enough to kill a potential sale. I had lots of instances in which people would read an early script of mine, give me a suggestion, and because of that, feel that they had the rights to it. There's a big difference between reading a script and giving notes and actually writing the script. But, because they had a meeting with me, they thought they were the producers of the project.

"Just remember — no contract, no money. You don't have to be grateful just to have met a producer or an executive. Beginning writers are so excited to be in the room with someone that they get taken advantage of along the way. So, the producers want a free option, and the writer might be tempted to do that. An option of $5,000 is a pittance to someone in this business, and it's not too much to ask for in a script option. If they can't come up with that, they're not really in the business."

Goyer reminded writers that the script is getting the attention, not you. There's no personal investment or feelings of responsibility. They don't care about you, so you shouldn't feel like you owe them anything special. In fact, since the town is so heavy on hype, and too often the subject of the hype doesn't sell. Then the script doesn't sell, and they don't return your call. All of that wonderful attention and flattery you earned originally means nothing then because you can't make a profit for them anymore — until you have another script. The spec script is commerce and money. It's what they trade in — or would like to trade in every day... There'll always be another spec script, and you can be forgotten tomorrow. Again, always keep in mind that this a business — not a grand, noble artistic pursuit.

"The script is the coin that agents and producers trade in — their currency. Because it takes up to six months to write a script, you should be careful about what you're writing and who you're giving it away to any time you submit it," Goyer added. "I've talked to a lot of beginning writers, and I know the kind of excitement or desperation they have inside them all the time. For most writers, those first few scripts are bad. They certainly were for me. It takes a while to become a good writer. You have to take years to break in out here. You have to have the fortitude or tenacity to keep at it. There's a lot of chance or luck involved as well. A lot of good scripts don't get sold, and a lot of mediocre scripts go because the timing was right. Of course, later on — after you make a sale — that script you didn't sell can find a home when those same people suddenly find out who you, the writer, are."

Goyer is right. It's always a question of taking the risk off of you. When you're a first-time writer, you're a risk because no one heard of you yet. The agent or producer is afraid to put his or her career on the back of an unknown writer, so your script really has to hit it out of the park. Once you have a sale under your belt, you're no longer a risk. Those same producers who turned you down before come back looking for what you might have on the shelf now. Of course, they're the same scripts you didn't sell before, but they end up looking a lot better from a known writer.

Goyer added, "If you look at the number of script or TV writers that are making a living, they're making about $80,000. That's good money, but it's not the significant amount of money that everyone dreams of out there. Still, there aren't that many people who are doing it, so anyone could break in if they keep at it long enough."

"I grew up in Michigan having never read a screenplay and knowing no one in Hollywood, and here I am. So, we have to come from somewhere."

That's great encouragement. But this isn't a book on inspiration. There are enough of those kind of writing tomes out there, if you want one. This is a work examining the hard decisions writers need to make as they are plotting their careers and writing their scripts. Still, you need to know how to come up with ideas that will sell in Hollywood, so we turn to someone who reads more high-concept scripts in a year than you have hot dinners.

Emile Gladstone

Hollywood is full of wonderful possibilities and hard truths. There are scores of people around town that are more than willing to tell you all about the former. The latter are a little hard to come by — unless you're fortunate enough to come across the refreshingly honest Emile Gladstone, literary agent with the highly successful Broder Webb Chervin Silbermann Agency.

For more than two decades, this powerful midsize house focused on "the long-term process of building and managing the careers of writers, directors, and producers." In 2002, BWCS sold a staggering 30% of the feature spec scripts and 20% of the feature pitches purchased in Hollywood. The agency had a string of hit movies either written, directed, or produced by its clients, including: *What Women Want*, *Hart's War*, *Pearl Harbor*, *Bring It On*, *Exit Wounds*, and *Dude, Where's My Car?* — with more on the way.

According to Gladstone, a winding road brought him to BWCS and his success as an agent. A 1990 graduate of Emerson College,

Gladstone originally came to Hollywood to be a writer. He managed to earn representation with the William Morris Agency during that time — gaining his initial insights into the inner workings of an agency and the writer/agency relationship: "I worked in production for a few years. I then took a job as an assistant at The Agency. After three weeks, I was made an agent when my boss left the firm."

After this first representation gig with The Agency, Gladstone headed to BWCS and, except for a brief stint at Michael Ovitz's AMG management firm, he's remained there ever since. He represents writers and directors for film. Some clients also work in television through other agents. BWCS enjoys a unique status in Hollywood. Bigger than a boutique and armed with an excellent representation for selling material and treating its clients well, the firm wields all of the power and success of a big house agency like ICM, CAA, or Endeavor without their massive operating costs and need to package writers with directors and actors. The agency employs more than twenty agents and handles only film and TV writers, directors, and producers — no actors. In fact, BWCS is the largest agency in Hollywood that does not handle on-screen talent. The firm also has a below-the-line division.

"The agency is well-respected in the community," Gladstone said. "That comes from the agents that work here. We work above board here — work against the cliché of what an agency is supposed to be. We work with people we respect because we're in the career business. We represent the best clients who are always out there working. They're professionals."

With all of the agency's success, the firm does not intend to push up into that rarified air of the so-called big houses: "We have no intention of growing to that size. Our overhead is less than that of the big houses. And, since this is a business, we make more money than they do because our expenses are lower."

"Where our clients are concerned, we know what war we're fighting for out there. It's the only place I could work doing what I do. It all starts with the writer. At big houses, the movie star and the director come first. He wanted to start a company where writers and writer/directors knew the agency's agenda was to sell a lot and get movies made for its clients. Our work speaks for itself, and the community knows that."

So, how do you, the aspiring writer, come up with ideas that get the attention of professionals at Gladstone's level? How should you proceed if you wish to gain the attention of the agents at BWCS? Should you approach an agent at a boutique or a manager? And what kind of high-concept idea do you need to develop while you're "alone in a room?"

First of all, Gladstone preaches an odd sort of Zen script marketing — and I agree with every word. Whether it's developing ideas, writing scripts, or marketing, consider the possibility that less is more — that the harder you tighten your fist, the more magic sand slips through your fingers. You need to rely on your story sense in developing Hollywood movies, and then be patient as you unveil those to the marketplace.

"First of all, approach nobody. Agents want to discover. They don't want to be discovered. So, get the Creative Directory. Read the trades. Contact the producers you find that are making the kinds of movies you want to write. I've never signed anyone off of a query letter. If you're sending letters, send them to producers. That can get you somewhere. Query letters to agents get tossed."

As far as what kind of scripts you should write before you get on that query letter merry-go-round, it's essential that you write good, high-concept, easy to pitch stories. Never target the marketplace. If disaster flicks are hot this week, they might not be by the time you are done writing one. But keep in mind what movies are selling out there in terms of simplicity and marketability. High-concept rules Hollywood, and that means agents, managers, or producers have to be able to see the poster and cut the trailer in their head before they buy the script or make the movie.

Do you want an example? "Three men battle a giant shark terrorizing a small island town." JAWS, obviously. And that concept gave birth to one of the great movie posters of all time with that shark's maw rushing up from the depths to swallow the naked blond. That's high concept. If you can envision all those elements of salability coming together for your movie, you're on the right track. In fact, I have one producer friend who is so tired of writers asking her what they should write to get sold that she immediately grabs the *LA Times* calendar section, opens it to the movie listings page, and shakes it in the questioner's face. Your movie better be able to find a place on that page, or the game's over for you before it even gets started.

Gladstone also encouraged aspiring writers to leave their artistic egos at the door: "If you see yourself as an artist who needs to express 'a voice,' you might write a good sample. But there're very few so-called 'voices' in Hollywood. Understand that the producers are looking for one-sheets. They have to be able to see the poster. So, if you're a comedy writer, write a broad comedy that could star a comedic actor. Write with marketing in mind — because people out here are reactive, and they react to what sells. Write a genre movie."

Now, pay attention. Gladstone's most important advice is coming up right here. It's so good I almost made it the title of this book, but "Alone in a Room" won the day. Still, if you have sense, you'll heed and obey...

"You always hear the cliché, 'Think outside the box.' In Hollywood, a writer should think inside the box. Hollywood is comfortable inside that box. Hollywood made that box. Hollywood needs the box. As a writer, it's your job to come up with something inside that box and make it fresh."

And it's best if you don't rely on your rep or anyone else to develop stories with you. Yes, if you're fortunate, you have a rep, mentor or other professional willing to give notes and advise on story development. But most pros in the ebbing and flowing stream of Hollywood material are looking for completed, ready to sizzle scripts. The legendary mantra at the William Morris Agency testifies to this demand for product with momentum: "Don't smell it. Sell it."

Once a writer breaks through with that workable project, Gladstone said he or she could make a healthy buck writing other producer's scripts for them.

"I represent a lot of writers who make a good living, but who have never sold a spec. Writing on assignment is the bread and butter of Hollywood, and the business will stay that way." (Don't worry. We go through that side of the writing business in a subsequent chapter.)

"So, don't express yourself like a grand artiste. Find nuances in your work, but surround those nuances with set pieces and trailer elements.

A good story has flairs of creativity, but you need to write a good movie that works in the marketplace."

A thought strikes me now. Between my musings and the square-jawed insights of Gladstone, we've taken a look at many of the challenges facing a lonely writer. But we haven't talked to any other writers yet. So, before I bring this chapter to a close, I wanted to include a couple of writer interviews to give you a glimpse into the mind of someone who sits... alone in a room (You're going to get sick of reading those four words, aren't you? Sorry.) and cranks out stories for the Hollywood machine. I chose these writers because they are as different as night and day — a big-time Hollywood powerhouse, a sensitive, sensual feminist playwright and academic turned screenwriter, and a former college football player turned badass Hollywood scribe. One writes for the art-house crowd, while the other is deep into the studio system. Between the two of them, they'll give you a good head start on the activities and philosophies of a working writer.

Erin Cressida Wilson

Erin Cressida Wilson does indeed work alone. There's no writing partner or editor looking over her shoulder or reviewing her writing. Her solitude is essential to her work as it examines very personal and powerful issues. In this overly sensitive and often pretentious age, it's not often that you hear an artist say that he or she creates original work especially to confront the restrictions of rampant political correctness. But that's one of the inspirations that screenwriter/playwright Erin Cressida Wilson cites as an original motivation and sustaining force in her provocative and challenging work.

An internationally produced and award-winning screenwriter, playwright, and professor at Duke University, Wilson saw her film

(*Secretary*, starring James Spader and Maggie Gyllenhaal) achieve significant critical success and several awards, including the coveted Special Jury Award at the 2003 Sundance Film Festival.

"I've been a playwright for fifteen years in New York City and San Francisco," Wilson said. "My work often centers around three-dimensional, complex, highly-sexed women."

Her personal interests and talents stretch beyond drama to the realm of song and dance as her musical, *Wilder*, opened off-Broadway at the Playwrights Horizons in 2002. The music was by Red Clay Rambler Jack Herrick (winner of a 1999 Tony Award) and Mike Craver. A native of San Francisco, her latest play, *I Feel Love*, is currently running at Campo Santo at the Intersection in San Francisco. Wilson premieres all of her new plays with Campo Santo and has garnered awards from the Bay Area critics and DramaLogues in this venue (including Best New Play of 1999).

Though she still has affection for her Bay Area roots, she cites the political hypersensitivity of the highly liberal and activist region for driving her on to bigger challenges.

"Obviously, challenging characters and subject matter interest me because I grew up as a writer in the 1980s in San Francisco," Wilson explained. "It was a very freeing environment, but also very politically correct and difficult to get work. I wanted to write about highly sexed, feminist women who also loved men. That's what motivated me to write. In the San Francisco environment, a lot of that subject matter was reserved for gay men. In my work, I want to suggest that it's possible to be a three-dimensional woman who loves men."

Wilson carried such characters into her critically acclaimed off-Broadway productions. The first was *The Erotica Project* (co-written with Lillian Ann Slugocki) at Joseph Papp's New York Shakespeare Festival. That play is now a book and has been produced theatrically all over the country. Another play, *The Trail of Her Inner Thigh*, was produced at the Labyrinth Theater (under the watchful eye of artistic directors Phillip Seymour Hoffman and John Ortiz). It is currently in development as a film with the Mark Taper Forum/Showtime series.

"I believe a writer must stay true to what drives them. I insist on writing characters who are complex and don't fall in a neat political niche. They have feelings that don't always line-up and don't comfortably fit with people's expectations." In fact, Wilson continued to defy politically correct expectations with *Secretary*, an adaptation of the darkly humorous short story, "Bad Behavior," by Mary Gaitskill.

In *Secretary*, a young woman discovers her own unique brand of love that frees her from the confines of the past and the deeply rooted expectations of others. Suffering from harmful obsessive behaviors, the story's heroine lands a secretary's job in a small-town law firm. She develops a crush on her older boss — who, once enraged by her mistakes, bends her over his desk and spanks her while she reads an error-ridden letter aloud. This outrageous assault is at once terrifying, humiliating, and strangely exciting for Lee. A humorous sadomasochistic relationship develops, eventually overwhelming them both.

Directed by Steven Shainberg and produced by Shainberg, Andrew Fierberg and Amy Hobby, the film provided Wilson with a challenge. As a screenplay, the short story had the danger of becoming just another "woman being made a victim," Wilson said. "I didn't want that as the short story has a beautifully written take on the secretary/boss cliché. The film became more than a tale on the lessons of men abusing women — but a complex examination of love and interaction."

Wilson will continue to work on a couple of screenplays on assignment for independent projects in New York. She also has a monthly sex column in *Razor* magazine and is completing her first novel about a unique sexual awakening in late 1970s San Francisco.

Sheldon Turner

While it's assumed that good writers possess some great, ethereal gift, working screenwriter Sheldon Turner insists that temperament is more important that raw ability. As I suggested before, it's hard-nosed business sense as much as creative ability that keeps a writer going in Hollywood.

"Temperament is more important than talent. Having the right attitude and nature is essential for a writer," Turner said — backing me up without even knowing it. An in-demand screenwriter, Turner has written for Columbia Pictures, Intermedia Films, Warner Bros., Universal, Lions Gate Films, MGM, and Dimension Films thus far during his career. On the television side, he developed projects for Fox, Touchstone, and USA Network.

After attending Cornell, where he played varsity football, Turner came out of law school at NYU in 1998, though he had no intention of ever practicing law: "I finished because I had a mother who would have kicked my ass if I hadn't done so. But I knew I wouldn't practice."

Turner uses his athletics experience when describing his transition into a screenwriter. He first enrolled as a quarterback at the University of Virginia. However, his first day on the practice field, he saw his competitors throwing 80-yard frozen ropes down the gridiron: "What was I doing there? I had a similar experience on my first day of law school. I looked around at the people surrounding me and knew I would never practice law."

Following law school, Turner headed to a San Francisco law firm for an internship: "I was bored out of my mind. There was nothing for me to do, so I would spend the morning reading newspapers — something I still do. But I knew I enjoyed writing, so after I sold a short story to the New Yorker, I decided to give screenwriting a shot."

"I saved money from my internship and came to L.A. I rented a single room, tended bar three nights a week, and I wrote. I have friends who continue to work the day job and write at night, and that's the most disciplined way to go about this life."

"I think I was drawn to the writer's life because I knew it was about me more than it was about the environment. The psychology was self-challenging. That worked for me. I wanted to get better at writing because it mattered to me. Just as I once dedicated myself to being a pro football player, I was able to take the same dedication to becoming a writer."

"I realized I would never run a 4.4 40, no matter what I did. But that moment never came to me in writing. Because I would read million-dollar scripts and say, 'Are you kidding me? Bring it on. Give me a shot at that.' The competitiveness came through there. That first script I wrote was crap, but it was a rite of passage. After that, I wrote fifteen scripts that no one ever saw. I kept at it — writing a new script every month that never went anywhere. The end game was to improve — to get better as a writer. That is what I mean by temperament. You need to be that patient and that dedicated to getting better."

"There's no substitute for tenacity — or maybe it's stupidity. Maybe you need to be too dumb to quit. But some of the greatest moments of my life were me sitting alone with a legal pad. That's not normal to most people, but it's essential to writers."

Turner is right when he suggests that people in the 9 to 5 world wouldn't understand the life of a writer — driven by guilt and fear. In fact, there are very few professions that offer as much solitude, and as a result, as much of a need to keep oneself motivated.

"You need the ability to handle the cabin fever — to take your shots, get kicked in the jaw, and still be able to delude yourself into going back and finding your answers on the page. Most of all, you need to be even-tempered. You'll get the asinine notes and meet miserable people. But that's not just Hollywood. You face those kind of issues in any business."

Now that Turner has spent a good amount of time settling into his life as a successful writer, he clearly values his craft: "I think screenwriting is the modern version of poetry — when it's done right. And too often it's thought of as 'anyone can do it.' But most people don't know what good writing is. What I find more than anything is the dearth of a voice. If you work for the studios, you can lose the voice or let them take your voice. But just as I can tell a great guitar solo, I should be able to tell a writer from the voice I'm seeing on the page."

According to Turner, the clearest echo of a good writer's unique voice comes in the form of outstanding dialogue. He calls good dialogue "the 90-mph fastball of writing" and counts it among the key components of a good spec script.

Another key is the ability to get a reader's attention quickly and hold it: "Put yourself in the mindset of a producer looking at fifteen scripts every day. You need something that's going to jump off the page. Nixon had a plaque on his desk that read, 'If you grab them by the balls, the heart and mind will follow.' But there's a difference between good and just shock value. Anyone can throw out something to grab attention, but it has to work. The toughest thing about writing a spec is that you only have a second to grab attention, so subtle is not valued. Subtle is lost — which is too bad because good writing is often subtle."

As for what subject matter or genre a spec writer should choose, Turner admits it's tricky — especially for writers who can do the small, artistic scripts well while looking to turn out something high-concept.

"The most dangerous thing for a writer is to be able to write the good popcorn movie and the subtle piece. But you need to face that as a writer and not get frustrated with it. It's too easy to blast Hollywood, but it's a commerce business. Maybe you should stretch yourself and try to get out of your comfort zone. Your anger at Hollywood might be anger at yourself for not being able to adapt.

"People in the business aren't there to validate you or make you happy. You're a cog in a wheel, like everyone else out here. You can complain, but why focus on that? Focus on getting the writing done."

Onward.

So, how's that for an initial chapter? Illusions shattered. Career paths explained. Writers analyzed. Sex. Sports. Mentions of Richard Nixon and men's groins. What else is there? Plenty. From here, we'll move on to examine the little-discussed world of working as a screenwriter on assignment.

Shock and awe.

chapter two

Should You Choose to Accept It:
Tips for Writers on Assignment

Ever since the early 1980s and the very green salad days of multi-million dollar spec sales and overnight miracle successes, the spec script has become the Holy Grail of the writing business. It's been said many times, but whereas writers used to slave away to produce the great American novel, they now aspire to that blockbuster spec screenplay. No matter where you are across the country, you come up with a great idea, write the golden spec, sell it, see it produced, and live happily ever after. That worked for Shane Black back in the days of *Lethal Weapon*, but times and the business changed. You want proof? Off the top of your head, name the last flash success writer who made the million-dollar spec sale and exploded into the pop culture consciousness? Right. I can't think of one recently, either — and I cover the business for a living.

Instead of viewing your spec sales as the end game of your career plan, perhaps envision them as just another step in your strategy. Your spec scripts are the calling cards introducing you to the industry. They get you read by agents and managers. They get you meetings with producers and directors. And, hopefully, they get you writing assignments.

The Real Gold Mine
It's a little known fact outside Hollywood that most working writers

in town make their living writing other people's ideas for them. Here's how it works. You initially write your spec scripts to get the attention of an agent or manager. I know that is in itself a tall order. I even wrote a book about how tough that can be. It's like the old Steve Martin joke in which he described how to be a millionaire and never pay taxes. First step? "Get a million dollars." Whether you get that first representation through a spec query or through an interested producer who calls an agent to do the deal for you, that first shopped script should pin down a negotiator for you.

With an agent or manager in your fold, you begin writing new specs with his or her assistance — hopefully, high-concept, market-friendly scripts that'll get read anywhere in town. When that material's ready, you have to endure the "script take-out." No, that isn't some weird Chinese dish for writers. (With two brads, you get egg roll?) Your agent or manager announces that the firm is taking your script out in the next day or so. They explain the genre and concept — maybe even throwing out a log line. They attempt to bait the hook for would-be buyers and get them salivating over your purified literary genius. Via messenger and shipping services, your script goes wide across town. And, as the writer, you must endure 72 hours of hell if it doesn't sell — and most don't. I speak from experience. The first day, you're sure it's going to sell. This will be the one. Your scissors are ready. You ride the emotional roller coaster of unlimited possibilities to "... sorry... back to the drawing board..." within a brief three day span.

Could be Worse...

To digress for only a moment, I can share my favorite spec take-out nightmare story. This one didn't happen to me, but rather to a writer I interviewed for this book (Dan Dworkin, currently a staff writer at ABC). His agent takes out a spec script — not his first, but the script that seems to have the best shot for a sale at the time. Out it goes. That very same day, Dworkin's grandfather dies. So he has to hop an emergency flight back east to attend the funeral. Once he's back home and riding with his parents to the funeral itself, he gets a call on his cell phone.

It's Dworkin's agent: "We have an offer on the script."

Now, Dworkin is in the back seat of his parents' car headed to a funeral for a beloved relative. So to suggest that there's suddenly a mix of emotions is a bit of an understatement. He merely asks his agent to keep him informed and continues his somber ride to the memorial services.

As he arrives at the cemetery, the agent calls again: "We've closed on the script." That means the deal is done. Dworkin apparently made his first spec sale while he was literally walking to graveside for internment of his grandfather. For obvious reasons, he decides not to say a word to anyone as this moment is a time of mourning centered around the memory of his relative.

However, at the wake after the service, Dworkin thinks perhaps his good news might lighten the mood and give the mourners a little bit of a lift out of their despair. So, he shares the big scoop, and everyone is immediately thrilled — insisting that his grandfather would be so proud of him. The wake soon changes to not only a celebration of Dworkin's accomplishment, but also a more upbeat retrospective on the grandfather.

In the middle of all that joy and nostalgia, Dworkin's agent calls again: "They reneged."

"What?!"

"They pulled out of the deal. I'm trying to get a hold of them for more details. I don't know what happened."

Now, understand... This never happens. Never. It is considered horribly unprofessional to pull out of a deal after negotiations closed on a sale. It is simply not done, and word of it will get around town if you pull something like this. Career suicide.

But that fact doesn't help Dworkin who now must wrestle with the truth that he unwittingly just lied to a room full of mourners. What could he do? Tell them the truth he just discovered and bring down the room with crashing bad news? Instead, he kept it to himself and broke the news to his folks some time after the funeral. Fortunately, the story eventually sold to a second buyer a couple weeks later, so the agony was short lived.

Whatever happens to you when you take your first story out into the world, I doubt your adventure will be anything like Dan Dworkin's. Mine certainly was nowhere near so dramatic. I thank Dan for the story.

From Heat to the Fire

Even if your spec doesn't sell, you're hoping it generates a little heat for you. You want producers, studio people, and development executives to desire the grace of your presence in meetings. They all have stories they're trying to develop into movies, and they need writers to do the deed. Rather than seeing your spec visions become legendary films, the more realistic career goal would be to pine for these precious writing assignments.

When writing on assignment, your job is to satisfy whomever hired you. It's not like when you work on your own specs and satisfy yourself and your creative vision. You have to meet the conditions of the assignment. It's really no different than if you accept an article assignment from a magazine or a ghostwriting assignment on a book. You must get the piece the producer or publisher envisioned to them when the work is finished. Obviously, the company that hired you to write the spec wants your input and your slant on the material. They wouldn't have hired you, otherwise. But if they want a by-the-numbers mystery thriller, you'd best not deliver a tense, pensive drama — even if all your instincts say that's what the story calls for in execution. You can make your case to the company paying for the script, but if their final decision goes against you, it is your professional responsibility to make certain you deliver what they want when they want it.

For additional takes on the rigors of writing for Hollywood on assignment, we again turn to professional, consistently working writers for their experience and insights into the realities of working on assignment. These folks are making their living (and a sizeable living it can be) writing scripts for the studios. They may indeed work on their own specs in hope that one will sell soon, but the bulk of their writing day is spent writing for someone else and using their creative energy to pull down an honorable check.

April Blair

With all of the social cache and intellectual worship the New York independent film scene generates, it's often advisable to lighten up a little to pay the bills as a screenwriter. April Blair, one of the hotter romantic comedy writers in Hollywood, found that out the hard way after college.

"I was an English major in college at the University of Miami, taking some writing classes — but not screenwriting. I wanted to be in the film industry, but I didn't know what any of the jobs were. I had sisters who worked in the film business, so I did a lot of PA work out of college. I worked my way up to production managing, but I still wanted to write. I teamed up with someone and started writing really dark and indie material. I was struggling, living in New York in that indie scene — trying to write those indie kind of movies."

During her time in New York, Blair worked with a writing partner. Although that original screenwriting partnership was not enormously successful, it did leave her with important insight on how to collaborate. By necessity, the process forces a writer to open up about his or her work.

"Some writers try to play it 'close to the vest' by not putting things in writing and keeping it in their own head. People get very possessive of their work and I don't think that is always a good thing because writers get a form of tunnel vision when it comes to their material."

About three years ago, Blair moved to Los Angeles and decided to get away from the gloom and doom: "I decided to go with the stuff I loved — corny '80s comedies like *Spies like Us* or *Overboard*. I embraced the corniness and stopped trying to be cool. About a year and a half ago, things started breaking, and every few months now, something is happening."

Blair sold three consecutive specs, including *Major Movie Star* to Warner Bros., *Operation Spy Girl* to Universal and *Double or Nothing* to New Line. She was also recently hired on assignment to adapt the bestselling Janet Evanovich book, *One for the Money*, with Jennifer

Lopez interested. The book tells the story of an out-of-work lingerie buyer turned female bounty hunter.

"It's light housewife reading, but it's fun. The character gets involved in finding her purpose, and it's very funny. The last four projects have definitely been of the 'chick flick' variety. But I do think that I will stay in that genre. I think I might like to extend to teens or male-driven stories, but I would stay in comedy. I just knew that those comedies were the kind of movies I enjoyed. I had a divorced childhood, and spent a lot of time moving around. So, maybe those sillier movies were a comfort for me. Living in New York and working in that dark, hipster scene, I was always the first person in line for the next romantic comedy — not telling my friends because it wasn't cool."

Now that Blair has found her comfortable genre, her writing process is based primarily on forced discipline: "It's a case of me trying to force myself to sit down and do the work. I outline a lot — spending a lot of time thinking about the story and working it out with index cards. The story is all worked out before I sit down to write. Once in the revision stage, it's a matter of sitting down and plowing throu the story until it's working thoroughly."

When it comes to rewrites of sold spec scripts, Blair must work with Warner Bros. and different studios. She is very careful to make sure the development executives see what they want to see.

"You take the studio's notes and implement them — showing them that they're in place. After note sessions, I like to write out all of the changes we agreed on so I can show those to the executives. I want the studios to see that last to make sure everyone is on the same page before I sit down to revise. That surprises them because other writers take notes and vanish. The execs are pleasantly surprised that I wanted to submit notes in outline form and include them in the process. I don't think many writers do that — go back and create a blueprint for the rewrite to make sure that's what everyone has in mind. Maybe it's a crutch just for me."

Blair explained that the development professional seem to be impressed by a well-organized writer: "It's odd that they're mesmerized by good pitches, but a little caught off-guard by organization because a good writer would seem to me to be better at the latter as part of the job."

Beyond organization, Blair believes the most important factor in revising is being open to changes: "I learned early on not to be too attached to any one version or vision of a story because I had to allow for how the person I was writing with (her then-writing partner) saw the script."

"That ability to compromise with my writing has helped me enormously when it comes to receiving notes from studios and producers. Sure there are things that I regret being too accommodating about in revision, but most of the time I'm pleasantly surprised by what people add to the process. There is a middle ground between being bullied and being bull-headed when you start in on the development process. And I'm always trying to find that middle ground."

Harris Goldberg

Let's stay in the comedy genre and examine another writer's difficult experiences writing on assignment. Why stay with this genre? Well, not only is writing a comedy difficult — perhaps the more most difficult of all genres — imagine having to write a comedy for the specific talents of a particular comic actor. The job forces a writer to find extra reserves of patience and discipline. Just ask Harris Goldberg, the successful comedy writer and director, whose recent credits include *Deuce Bigalow* with Rob Snyder and *The Master of Disguise*, starring Dana Carvey.

In both cases, Goldberg co-wrote the scripts with the star who would eventually appear on screen. The projects were specifically created for Snyder and Carvey respectively, so the screenplays had to play to their strengths — while also incorporating all of the essential elements present in any successful script.

"I met Rob Snyder as a friend," Goldberg said. "We ended up hosting the Montreal Comedy Festival together and appearing on Conan O'Brien, but Rob would say what a tough time he was having getting anything going in Hollywood. Around that time, I rented *American Gigolo* with Richard Gere and started joking about Ron starring as a gigolo. He thought that was a great idea and asked me to write it for him. I went off and wrote some other movies, but I cranked out about twenty pages on the idea. It was really funny, so we took the idea to Adam Sandler, who had just started his production company and was looking for a project. Adam backed it, and the film did well."

After Goldberg finished the Snyder project, Todd Garner (of Revolution) called and suggested that Goldberg help in creating a project to resurrect the movie career of Dana Carvey: "I met with Revolution, and they had something they wanted him to do, which I didn't really like. I wanted to meet Dana and get to know him. So, we just spent some time laughing and getting to know his characters. The original idea for *Master of Disguise* came from that.

However, Revolution didn't want to do that film. To convince the people at Revolution, Goldberg and Carvey took an older film, *My Name is*

Nobody, and cut Carvey into its scenes as a demonstration. The result drew enough laughs for Revolution to green-light *Master of Disguise*. Now all Goldberg had to do is find a way to work with Carvey and get the film written.

Goldberg can offer unique insight that you're not likely to find in too many other places. This guy writes with comics in the room — hovering nearby and guiding the writing process. He not only has to write to the studio's desires; he has to keep the star of the would-be film happy during the creative work.

"When you're dealing with talent, they're pretty mercurial with their opinions and emotions. You have to observe. They have good days and bad days. So, I have to be the stabilizing force. These stars have a style you have to get used to, and you create a story to fit them. They're good at sketches and jokes, but I have to show them how the through-line and plot-points are necessary. You almost have to have a dramatic storyline, and hang the jokes onto that."

Goldberg credits his brother, Danny, with some of his comic writing insights. Danny wrote the Bill Murray hits of the '70s and '80s, *Stripes* and *Meatballs*.

"Those movies that my brother wrote taught me a lot about structure, and I think a lot of the very similar and often unsuccessful comedies out there suffer due to a lack of that structure."

Once Goldberg had the overall structure of *Master of Disguise* in place, it was time for Carvey to play: "The fun part of working with talent is that you have the characters right there in front of you. When you write for a specific actor, you know whom you're writing for as you write it. The problem is that they want to put every one of their jokes in the movie. I have to act as a diplomat and say, 'Yeah it's funny, but it doesn't really fit in this movie.

"I would usually sit at the computer and type, while Dana walked around and acted out the bits. It helps a lot if you're working together on an individual script. To capture those moments."

However, Goldberg lamented that the film changed significantly after he and Carvey completed their original work: "Originally, when we wrote the first draft, it was an R-rated movie. The comedy was biting and edgy. I thought it was hilarious. Suddenly, the powers that be said that PG movies are 'in' now. Unfortunately, by doing that with this script, it took away the integrity of the story. From (the executives') points of view, it's 'Why can't you just take out this or that joke? Can we put in a kid? Can we put in a dog?' The original idea was, 'Let's do a story adults will like that kids will watch for visuals, et cetera.' It gets skewed to what the business guys want. I think this project suffered for it."

The fact that *Master of Disguise* bombed and was named one of the worst films of the year by some critics didn't help to brighten Goldberg's mood regarding the project. So, you see, even a writer as successful as Goldberg (a man who is already where you want to be) faces highs and lows — creative thrills and disappointing frustrations. The quest to do better work, to develop better projects, and to drive one's career stays with you — even when you're already an established writer and working on assignment for the studios.

As screenwriter Ed Solomon once said, "Writing for Hollywood is either the greatest shit job in the world, or the shittiest great job in the world."

bonus chapter

The Challenges of Adaptation

Now, there are entire books dedicated to the art of adapting novels or short stories into screenplays. I lack the page count here to go into the entire process in significant detail. However, it is a key segment of the assignment-writing field. Producers and studio executives looking to adapt material face multiple challenges. They have to find a writer who can compose a competent screen story, obviously. But they also need someone who has an understanding and sensibility for the material. If a writer has a flare for *Jane Eyre* – style period pieces, they're not going to prove an attractive choice for an Elmore Leonard adaptation.

How do you indicate that you have the chops to write novel, short story or even graphic novel adaptations? Again, Zen comes into play. You try by not trying. You write the marketable specs you feel comfortable writing. If you're drawn to a specific genre or style of writing, write it. In time, if that style meets a good adaptation candidate, it should prove a happy marriage. If you find a flare for writing period dialogue, that ability might find a home some time down the road with the adaptation of a play or classic novel. So, hone your ability and worry about what comes of that work later.

In the meantime, let's have a chat with writers who not only worked on adaptations, but who had to deal with some major authors — powerful literary figures whose work demanded a certain level of professionalism.

Todd "Kip" Williams

It seemed like a one-in-a-million shot and took a while to come together, but persistence and a willingness to work on faith brought Todd "Kip" Williams and master novelist John Irving together. Following the success of the Oscar-winning *The Cider House Rules*, which pulled down an Academy Award for Best Adapted Screenplay for Irving, a small bidding war broke out for the rights to adapt Irving's latest bestseller, *A Widow for One Year*. The novel starts in 1958 with a couple shattered by the deaths of their sons in a freak car accident. The husband, seeking to prompt a divorce, hires an assistant who is a dead ringer for one of the sons, leading to the wife's strangely incestuous affair with him. She leaves her husband and her daughter, and the tale goes in different directions over the next forty years.

How did the project come to rest at the feet of a relatively unknown, yet talented writer and filmmaker like Williams, the director of the low budget *The Adventures of Sebastian Cole*? How did Williams seize the opportunity of his artistic lifetime without a dollar changing hands? Williams was able to persuade Irving to grant him the rights to develop the book for no money after the filmmaker impressed the author with his version of an adapted screenplay. Several writers wrestled with how to adapt the elaborate novel. The task of distilling the story down to a tighter, cinematic format baffled most of them. Williams concocted a functional plan of how to boil down a book as packed with dysfunction and tragedy as Irving's *The World According to Garp*. New York-based Good Machine was completing fundraising as this piece went to press. Williams' partner Ted Hope, who is producing the film, met Williams while he was editing *Sebastian Cole* and wanted to be involved in the follow-up, even if he thought he hadn't a prayer to get the rights to such a popular book.

"It seemed a most unlikely follow-up to a no-budget film, because *Cider House Rules* was just coming out and John Irving is one of America's best-selling authors," Hope said.

However, Hope was in a position to get Irving to take a meeting. Irving was briefly Hope's high school wrestling coach at Exeter College. Good Machine also completed two movies with *Cider House* star Toby McGwire, who made introductions all around. Irving didn't care as much about getting paid for his book right away and wasn't put off by the filmmakers' lack of credits after he watched *Sebastian Cole* and saw that Williams had figured out a way to film what is in and of itself a tough literary adaptation. Irving first met with Ted and Kip at his home in Vermont. After the initial meeting, it became clear that all three men shared a common vision for the first section of the novel's extended story.

Williams explained that he always imagined a film of only the first part of the novel, only up to the wife leaving her husband and daughter behind, after her affair with the prep school boy.

"When I read the end of that first section, I just saw it as a movie, I saw an opportunity to do some of the things I attempted to do in my first film, and hoped I would get the opportunity. I didn't even think the chance would really come about and I didn't look on developing the adaptation as work because it seemed like a long shot, but it turned out to be an easy mountain to climb — a reasonably smooth ride. It was a great project to work on and to watch come together."

Williams expected Irving would reject such a radical reduction of his novel, but the author quickly warmed to the idea. Apparently, early ideas for making *A Widow* all pointed to the end of the story, with the murder of a prostitute in Amsterdam, a Dutch policeman's investigation, and other intrigue. Williams wasn't interested in the thriller aspect of the novel and only wanted to examine the more human story told in the earlier pages. Williams left the meeting with a deal to write the script, the first draft of which completely won over the author. Throughout this process, no one discussed money. Irving sought little to allow Williams to begin his adaptation, while Williams asked for none for his chance to adapt the book. Instead, Williams did what too few professional writers do. He stopped worrying about dollars and cents and simply wrote the script. Irving writes his novels the same way. He doesn't pitch ideas and then negotiate a fee. He finishes a book, and then allows his agents to sell it.

So Irving respected Williams' enthusiasm: "What I liked about Kip from the start was that he was willing to write the script and show it to me and see what I thought. So many screenwriters come to me and say, 'Do you like my idea? Will you back it? ' Ideas are worthless to me. The writing is what counts."

Williams was drawn to Irving's novel because of its blunt, shocking material — the sort of ground Irving usually covers in his work: "I wanted to explore that darker material in a more human way. I want to focus on the rich characters Irving always provides, and not as much the complex plot. The novel is so huge that I think it's best to look at those characters and early events without trying to encompass the entire story."

Williams continually met with Irving, who remained an active partner in the project: "He's very busy, but he's very generous and very supportive. I was envisioning him as one of the most accomplished living novelists, but from the beginning, he treated me like an equal. I think of him as a friend — someone I can always go to when I have questions."

So, would you be up to the challenge of adapting the work of one of the great novelists of this era — even if he himself signed off on you as a choice for the project? As Williams demonstrates, the key elements to surviving such a challenge are hard work, confidence, and passion for the overall project. In such a case, your spec scripts would have got you to the dance. If the reader of those pieces believe you're up to it, don't argue with him. Put your butt down in that chair and write. That is your first, best course of action during adaptation.

Meanwhile, our next interview offers yet another daunting confrontation with pressure. If the possibility of adapting the work of John Irving doesn't scare you enough, how would you like to sit down across from perhaps the greatest American playwright of the twentieth century and tell him how you plan to take one of his classics to the screen?

Jesse Wigutow

Having interviewed more than my share of writers over the years, this author thought he had heard it all when it came to the professions men and women worked in before emerging as Hollywood professionals. They were writing assistant, legal word processors, security guards, dog walkers, studio tour guides, et cetera. However, Jesse Wigutow, writer of *Urban Townie* and adapter of Arthur Miller's classic play, *The Ride Down Mount Morgan*, managed to come up with easily the most unique occupation to date... Muppet fluffer.

"I graduated from Cornell as an English major, studying creative writing," Wigutow said. "After school, I got a job working on *Sesame Street*, essentially working as a muppet fluffer. I would move Big Bird around, plug feathers back in that fell out, whatever needed to be done."

After moving, repairing, and fluffing Muppets, Wigutow moved on to work for the *New Yorker* for a year as an assistant to the art director before leaving New York.

"I moved to Chicago to work on the CBS show *Early Edition*," he said. "While I was there, one of my jobs was to download all the scripts written in Los Angeles by the writers. I realized that I could do the writing. That level of work was not obtainable for me."

Off that experience, he applied to graduate film school and attended AFI the following year. After two years in the screenwriting department there, he had completed several projects, spending a lot of time alone in front of his computer. It paid off as he made his first sale a month or two after graduation with *Urban Townie*. "That launched my career. Within a couple weeks, Brad Pitt was attached to it, and we soon had a start date. Then it fell apart, got set-up again... That process seemed to repeat itself a few times. But it got me started. After *Urban Townie*, I had a number of meetings. Every executive and production person wants to meet the new writer. Most of them are 'getting acquainted' meetings, and not a lot comes of it. But I took one meeting and got onto a project called *Kitchen Confidential*, based on a *New York Times* bestseller."

The research for the *Confidential* project was interesting as he got to work in New York City kitchens. But, his most compelling adaptation might be his work with the great playwright, Arthur Miller. "When I got to adapt *The Ride Down Mount Morgan*, I got to have lunch with Arthur Miller. That was somewhat surreal — sharing a large pizza with him. He was very lucid, very talkative and charming. He didn't really want to talk about the play much, which was okay with me, considering

I'd have to adapt it. Instead we got to talk about his life, his history in NYC, how it's changed, and such."

For that adaptation, it was difficult to expand a story that takes place primarily in a hospital room: "So, expanding Miller's work was surreal and farcical because it felt like, 'Who am I to be taking liberties with one of the century's great authors?'" However, Wigutow overcame that inferiority complex quickly — as every professional must.

Since then, he has written both his own specs and on assignment. "I try to maintain a practice of doing both kinds of work, and I'd like to keep doing that as long as I can." His biggest spec sale to date was *Runs In the Family* with Hollywood legends Kirk and Michael Douglas. Wigutow based much of that story on his own family experience.

"Last summer, after being on set during *Runs in the Family*, I was feeling like being more a part of the process. I have a script that I've been writing that I would like to direct. I still feel like I have a lot to learn on the directing front before I tackle a feature. But, I would like to direct at some point — if that's not too much cliché."

For now, Wigutow is happy to write. He keeps the pages piling up with determined discipline. Just how does he get the work done while he's alone in a room?

"I do a lot of outlining to begin with because it's important to have an idea where you're going. You need to know where the end point of this story you're trying to write is. Even if it changes, you have an idea of where you're going and where the process will take you. So, doing your homework earns you the right to bang out the draft."

As for research, the amount and procedure varies from project to project: "For the kitchen project, I worked in a kitchen for a couple of weeks. It was easy to get a sense of the language and culture. The rest was making a story out of it. For my next project (a factual drama on the inner workings of the pharmaceutical industry), I could have done a year's worth of research, but I finished that phase after four months. The more I did, the more I felt I was losing the broader sense of the story because details can mask the broad strokes. It cornered me into narrative spaces that didn't help me out, so it was time to move on. I'm all for reality and veracity, but you can cut a corner or two to make sure that story works. The story is the king."

During the writing stage, Wigutow likes to go to a space (public library or his office), where he can keep banker's hours: "I try to write all day — maybe not typing, but staying in that space. I might throw in a nice extended lunch break. I'm definitely a day writer — not a night owl. I like to be able to put it away at the end of the day."

"What I'm drawn to is generally character-driven stories that are not very funny. I'd like to write something funny, but I don't know if I have it in me. I think dramatic character pieces and adaptations are what I'm drawn to instinctively, but it's not what I want to do forever."

So, while a writer at Wigutow's level has the luxury to plan ahead and consider moving beyond adaptation, that may be the kind work you aspire to attack one day. Between now and then, focus on making your spec script as strong as you can — even if that means taking difficult revision notes on your script.

Protect yourself from hostile attacks.

chapter three

Everybody's a Critic:
Dealing with "Notes"

You can't escape notes. You get them during story pitches. You get them while you're writing a first draft. You get them after you hand in a first draft. You get them before and after a revision. You get them from other writers, producers, agents, managers, friends, enemies, relatives, taxi drivers, janitors, and homeless people (including agents who lost their jobs for giving too many bad notes). The reason you get so many opinions from so many different angles is because (and I am not the first writer to stumble upon or suggest this fact) everyone in the entertainment business thinks they're creative. It doesn't matter if they work in the accounts department or spend their time filing as a coordinator in the visual effects department. They think they have the creative instincts and abilities of a writer.

It's not really fair, is it? Writing remains one of the only professions in which people who can't do what you do see fit to judge what you do. I suppose football coaches have to put up with this sort of nonsense during Monday morning quarterbacking. But surgeons don't have packs of strange people watching over their shoulders criticizing how they made that stitch during wound closure. Architects don't have to weather criticism because they decided not to use a flying buttress on their most recent cathedral design. But anyone who even glanced a keyboard in passing at the office supply store or who wrote a grocery list knows what kind of story you need to tell and how you should tell it.

So the trickiest part of taking notes is never how to find them. It's deciding which notes are best to take seriously — and managing to fend off the foolish suggestions without looking like a howling jackass. I think the former challenge is fairly easy to grasp. You want to seek notes from Hollywood professionals who work with stories on a regular basis, or other writers whose abilities you respect. There are some people out there who advertise themselves as story gurus, and they charge money to break down and analyze your work. I don't have an overwhelming amount of respect for most of them. To me, too many of them seem like bottom feeders who skulk about looking to make money off of overeager, starving writers. There is one professional analyst I do respect (Meg LeFauve), and we'll meet her in detail in this chapter.

Of course, once you're making your living as a writer, you won't have to seek out people to give you notes. You'll get them from all sides — from people whose job it is to offer suggestions (development execs, story editors, et cetera.). Along comes the next challenge. How do you take notes (some of which can be insufferably off target) and keep a constructive smile on your face — i.e. not reach across the table and physically assault your way out of the business?

Fortunately, you immediately have one factor in your favor. I call it the Law of Hollywood Misbehavior. It reads: *There are enough first-class jag-offs in the entertainment industry (people who are naturally devoid of or who choose to discount civil and polite human interaction) that if you simply behave with basic human courtesy and consideration, you immediately ascend to "extremely classy" status.* In other words, average, polite human conduct in Milwaukee, Wisconsin or Beaver Valley, Utah would be considered angelic behavior in Hollywood. If this was an equation, it'd look something like this: (Standard) Courtesy = (Hollywood) Courtesy[3].

That law helps you look better during the note process if you just keep your head. There are umpteen screenwriting books out there that tell you that you must have a thick skin to survive in the business, so I won't repeat that. But you must never take creative criticism in the form of script notes as a personal assault — even the foolish notes (and, you will get those — trust me). Keep a smile on your face and maintain an open mind because you can often garner sound insight amidst all of the noise and haste.

Whether you're taking notes on a script you've written, pitching a new story and getting feedback, or getting someone else's take on a rewrite you did, you should take it all in with enthusiasm. So many writers think it's just enough to keep a positive attitude. For example, you shouldn't take every note with a sigh, grumble, and eye roll as if the commentator is either an idiot or some vicious attacker of your biblically brilliant work. Your story is not a child of your creation. It is product, and the critic is presumably giving you notes to improve that product.

Beyond merely tolerating the notes you get, you should engage in the give and take of the critique process with some excitement. It's group creativity in action — and it's that interaction or ebb and flow of ideas that you don't get while you're writing on your own alone in a room. Take their ideas and spin them into your own. Throw out questions to their questions as if you really want to explore what they have to say. First of all, you're showing professional courtesy. Second, they might actually have something to add.

And, let me repeat: The note process does not take place only when you've already written a script. You also get notes before beginning your work — especially during writing assignments in which you're paid to prepare a script for a producer based greatly on their vision and hopes for the project. And, notes come during a pitch.

A story pitch is self-explanatory. You literally pitch a story you'd like to write or the approach you'd like to take on existing material. If the producer or executive is receptive, the pitch takes shape from there based on their input. Hopefully, you don't get the deadly, stop sign note of "We're already doing something like that" or "That's not what we're looking for right now." You're looking for notes that are positive suggestions or questions. Even these notes can have the same psychological effect here in a pitch session that they have during a revision meeting. They can feel like a threat. They can frustrate you. They can even confuse you, but maintain an open mind when you're taking these notes. In fact, I think you should pay extra attention when notes are irritating because that upset might be there indicating that you have more work to do than you originally planned.

Meet the Reeves-Stevens... or Reeves-Stevenses... or Reeves-Stevensesesss...

Judith and Garfield Reeves-Stevens are the perfect people to explain how to handle notes amiably during a revision meeting or a pitch session. Why? Because just about everyone who meets them says they're far too nice to have found so much success in Hollywood. A mutual friend of ours once said they're the kind of polite, soft-spoken Canadians you'd expect to find running a bed-and-breakfast in Niagara — not writing screenplays, TV scripts, novels, and nonfiction books.

These people know notes, and they know how to take notes — because they take them all the time on such a wide variety of projects. A pair of *New York Times* bestselling novelists, their most recent novel, *Quicksilver*, is a prophetic thriller about a terrorist attack on the

Pentagon. It's a follow-up to the Canadian writing team's *Los Angeles Times* bestseller, *Icefire*. They conducted some of their research for *Icefire* during an expedition to Antarctica on assignment for Microsoft's "Wild Lit" series of adventure-travel articles for the Internet.

In TV, the Reeves-Stevenses were staff writers for the second season of *Sir Arthur Conan Doyle's The Lost World*, the syndicated one-hour action-adventure series from New Line. For the series' third season, the Reeves-Stevenses returned as supervising producers on location in Australia. In other episodic work, the Reeves-Stevenses have written for John Woo's *Once a Thief*, *The Hitchhiker*, MTV's *Catwalk*, and *Beyond Reality*. They have also developed television series with Dreamworks, Film Roman, Universal Television, Gary Goddard's Landmark Entertainment, the Edward R. Pressman Company, Alliance-Atlantis, Nickelodeon, and the Canadian Broadcasting Corporation.

In features, their commissioned script projects include the all-new adventure epic, *Journey to the Center of the Earth*, inspired by the Jules Verne novel and updated for the twenty-first century, for Richard Zanuck at Fox 2000; an original long form based on Edgar Allan Poe's "The Raven," for Arts & Entertainment/Nelvana; and a feature adaptation of the ongoing fantasy adventure series of novels and games, *Dragonlance*, for TSR/Nelvana. They're published in the United States, Canada, and England, and in translation in Czechoslovakia, France, Germany, Holland, Israel, Italy, Japan, Poland, Russia, Spain, and the Ukraine.

Now, this couple tends to talk tag-team style. No, they don't share a brain. In fact, they have extra brains sitting around the house that you might like them to share with you. But they do tend to complete each other's thoughts as they roll. So stick with me.

They began their discussion of how to handle notes by answering a common question. In the give-and-take of a note session, how do you maintain your focus? In other words, you're presenting your ideas — in the flow and discussing your story. Suddenly, there's a question from the peanut gallery. You take time to answer it. But how do you get back into your presentation?

According to Judith, "Every time someone in the room asks you a question during a meeting, it's an opportunity to sell them on your project more. They're asking you that question because they've found something in your story that interests them. And they're looking to see how you respond to the question. If you can respond to the question nimbly and turn it to your advantage, so that it is directed toward something that they think is a problem and diffuse it right away, that's the neat part. Because so and so is going to find out such and such, you can say, 'You're right. You got it. That's the question that's going to be in the audience's mind.' So you reward them and involve them in your creative process."

Garfield added, "As for memorizing your story for a notes session, I think that's a bad idea. We lose freshness. For example, what we've found is that best pitch sessions are conversations. You're not describing the story you want to write, the movie you want to make, or the episode you want to compose. You're telling your friend about a great show you already saw on TV last night. That whole idea of keeping it short is key because you're always trying to tell your story in a paragraph. If they want to hear more, you can tell an even longer version. But to sit down and recite your five-page story, that'll put the room to sleep."

"I think it's like one of those study techniques they teach you," Judith said. "You try to learn everything. Then you boil it down to an out-line. Then you write it down on index cards. Then it comes down to one word that acts as a memory device that unpacks the entire story. Don't give them details in a big loop because they don't know where it'll start and end."

I think that's key because one thing you don't want to do when you go into a room to do notes or pitch is bore the room. The people you're meeting with don't want to be read to or stifled during the work day any more than they already are. So, can you offer a respite? Can you energize and entertain them? Should they be happy to see you or should they dread your coming into the office? They don't know where you're going with your story, and the moment they think, "Oh, no. He's going to be long-winded and boring for the next half-hour," you've lost them.

Garfield agreed, "You have to be flexible and think on your feet. You tell the paragraph version of the story. And if the producer offers a note, 'Oh, if this story could be told in San Francisco, I have a perfect place for it,' you alter your presentation to fit. It gives you a chance to groove your story to their needs."

"When you're pitching, you're also practicing," Judith added. "You won't be going to just one meeting to pitch an individual story. You'll probably go to four or five meetings on that story. So, as you're pitch-ing and watching the reactions of your audience, you'll see that some-thing caught their interest — a phrase or a sentence. If it works again on the next room, that phrase should be in your pitch every time. It's like rehearsing a comedy routine. They do it over and over, night after night in the club. They discard what doesn't work and keep what does.

You might go into that first pitch with four or five sentences that you think will hook them. And you see which one of those work. And no two pitches will end up the same because you're getting notes from different people."

"A couple key phrases — that's something we always do," Garfield said. "And we get there by writing and rewriting a story. We start with a twenty-page version, and rewrite it as a ten-page story, then a five-page — then down to a single page. Finally, end up with that one succinct paragraph that really sums up the story. Having written it so many times, we know the story so well that we can work with the notes we get and still be able to perceive our story. It's almost as if you're writing your trailer or movie poster for them. And we know the executives want to see that poster and see that trailer. Everybody's hooked. You tell the stories in a couple of sentences. If you sense interest, you can go into the machinations of the story and work with whatever notes you get from there."

Also, I would add the tried-and-true strategy of poker to your presentation and interaction. No matter if it's a straight notes session or a pitch, keep an ace up your sleeve and play your cards close to the vest. You want the listener to be excited about your ideas for the story, but you don't want to unload every last insight you have. Tease them a little. Make them ask for more. If they hit on something cool, you've got them. Then, you unpack your best idea — showing off the twist you came up with in the story without telling them.

During all of this, what if you come across some truly brutal notes? I mean, these notes are stunningly stupid, spectacularly dim suggestions that would not only kill your story but would turn it into something you'd rather eat than write — all 110 pages of it. What do you do? You smile and pretend to consider them. Why? Remember the (Standard) Courtesy = (Hollywood) Courtesy[3] formula. Even if the notes session doesn't go well, you want the producer sitting there to like you and think highly of your professionalism so he or she will call you back in for a rewrite of something else (or just to pitch when you have other good stories down the road). No one wants to work with a jackass, and there are plenty of other people that producer can meet with if you should prove to be just such a pain. It helps if you have no expectations one way or the other when you enter a notes meeting because they never seem to go the way you're predicting anyway. Think on your feet and stay upbeat. You are on display as much as your written work.

Garfield agrees: "We tend to go into meetings with the goal of having a pleasant meeting so that the next time we want to pitch something, we can go back. And it's also your opportunity to know about them and learn what they do, what they like, and what their overall interests are."

So that gives you a good primer on how writers handle the notes process. It would help to understand notes from the other side of the desk. Our next interview subject makes her living developing stories, both as a producer and as a top story analyst and coach. She's read countless scripts, always on the lookout for the suggestion or the challenge she can make to push the work over the edge into that magical realm of a sure-fire sale. I include this upcoming section because it does you a huge favor by showing you what mistakes to avoid so you head off common notes before you need to sit through them.

Meg LeFauve — Storycoach

When you ask Meg LeFauve why a successful producer like herself would take the time out of her insanely busy schedule to work with aspiring, developing screenwriters, she's hesitant to answer: "I hate to say it because I know it sounds phony. But I love the development process — working with scripts and helping writers struggle through their story challenges until it all falls into place. That moment when the writer sees it all come together — that's why I do it."

LeFauve heads up her own film production company, One-Eyed Dog. Before founding that firm, she was President of Egg Pictures, Jodie Foster's film production company on the Paramount back-lot. A veteran producer who worked on such successful projects as *Nell*, *Home for the Holidays*, *Waking the Dead*, *The Baby Dance*, and *The Dangerous Lives of Altar Boys*, starring Vincent D'Onofrio and Foster, with animation sequences by *Spawn* creator, Todd McFarlane.

LeFauve started with Egg as a story editor and worked her way up to producer and president. Her love for stories and for the narrative development process guided her ten-year Hollywood journey and helped to develop her ability to analyze and improve screenplays in all genres. She is now a highly sought-after consultant, helping writers, directors, producers, and executives plug the holes in their narratives. Unlike many consultants, she doesn't actively seek clients. They come to her, and she must often turn them away simply because her schedule as a producer doesn't allow her to help as many writers as she might like. She offers her insights into the mistakes she sees most writers (both working professionals and aspiring apprentices) making on a regular basis.

First, LeFauve identified some general errors that often surface in discussions of weak scripts, such as vague act breaks and sloppy overall script structure. However, she offered unique personal observations you won't get from other story consultants who never produced a feature film: "Most often, an inexperienced writer's first act is mainly back-story. In other words, the movie doesn't really start until the script's page 20. That first act is useful as character back-story outside of the script, but audiences are too savvy for that. They want the movie to start."

LeFauve also warned writers not to make their main characters too reactive instead of proactive. She explained her belief that most writers are their main characters, and they essentially experience the story as it develops with their protagonists. In that sense, the narrative happens to the writers as it unfolds for their heroes and heroines.

"A hero needs to be active. He or she needs to take definitive action in the story by — at the latest — the script's midway point."

LeFauve pointed out that the best, most successful active characters act out of internal and external goals: "We're watching a story to see what the obstacles are to those goals. Often ineffectual characters have a very clear external goal, such as 'get the money,' but there's no internal emotional goal. There's nothing connected to that goal metaphorically. What does that money mean to them?"

In the plot department, LeFauve urged all writers to forge a sound, cause-and-effect story. She indicated that scribes too often string together a list of events and situations for convenience's sake: "Unfortunately, that doesn't make a good story. When events happen, they should directly influence the plot and its characters — never seeming incidental or random. That's the difference between describing a random situation and constructing a believable story. No writer should be able to stitch a character into a plot during Act One. In other words, that plot and its given character must be made for each other. They must need each other to work. At any moment in your script, your main character should not be able to stand up and say, 'I'm going to get on a bus and head to Mexico.' In that case, your story and your protagonist do not need each other to exist. The audience will sense that externally and internally because the character is not emotionally sewn into the fabric of the script."

As a producer, LeFauve stressed the "Why this character to this plot?" relationship because it's a key question good actors consider when reading a script. Since she worked with a two-time Oscar winner for years, LeFauve knows something about what actors look for in a story.

"As a writer, you need the actor to want to make your movie. Actors ask why their character is essential to the script. If the protagonist is a cop who will arrest countless crooks throughout his or her career, why is this particular criminal the one we're going to watch throughout the story? Why is the story going to crack open the main character like never before? That link between plot and hero is key for an actor."

In terms of overall concept, LeFauve (like Emile Gladstone earlier) warned writers not to try too hard to identify the latest trend: "It's a mistake to write a script because you think that's what Hollywood wants. In that case, there's nothing personal in it. The script will lack a personal POV on the world. There's nothing wrong with writing a big-budget, high-concept studio movie, but it's best to smuggle a little of yourself into the story."

In the end, LeFauve acknowledged that all writers work differently when they're alone in a room. Some hate creating outlines and choose to jump right to their keyboard, while others create elaborate flowcharts and several treatments before beginning a script. However, she urged writers to ask themselves some key questions. Her checklist included:

✓ What's the main character's external and internal goal?

✓ What characters constitute the main or essential relationship in your story?

✓ What's the tone of your story? If it's a comedy, is it broad and physical or dry and witty?

✓ What are your act breaks? You should be able to spot them and point them out easily.

✓ What's your story's climax? Does it fulfill your main character's needs?

✓ Who's the audience for your movie? To whom would you like to see your story marketed in theatres?

Obviously, those are just starting points, but LeFauve wished to offer them to interested writers with the hope that they might unlock those special moments she loves to see: "I enjoy working with a writer and seeing the light come on after he or she worked so hard and struggled so much. When that writer finally discovers whatever the key might be that allows all of the story elements to fall into place, it's a great feeling."

So, now that you have your "notes on notes," you have a better grasp on how to listen, how to handle them, and how to respond. However, once the notes are in and you have your direction pegged for a particular story, you're back where you started — alone in a room and facing a revision according to those notes. You've probably heard the old cliché that "writing is rewriting." We're about to find out just how true that is — whether you like it or not.

Be prepared.

chapter four

Get It Right the Second Time:
Executing Revisions

Without question, revision is the stage of writing that clearly and permanently separates the wannabe amateur from the dedicated professional. Sadly, it is also the phase of forging a written work that gets the least attention in most creative writing classes, screenwriting books, and screenplay workshops. Revision is the naked emperor — the pink elephant in the middle of the room that no one wants to acknowledge. Every screenwriters knows revisions are necessary, but few pros ever discuss them because rewrites are the slow, redheaded stepchild that the smart, skilled family of writers wants to deny exists.

Why do revisions get the brush-off? There's nothing sexy about them. No one thanks his or her muse after slaving over the same ten pages for two hours and striking out every occurrence of passive voice or dangling modifier. It's chic to discuss your latest screenplay at a party and all the related inspiration and glorious creativity, but your date's eyes will glaze over when you start droning on about how you had to amalgamate two characters into one because there wasn't enough for both of them to do before the third act break. I almost passed out while typing that last sentence. That's how tedious revisions can become.

However, detailed and through revision is essential if you intend to produce professional level work. If you're writing screenplays as a diversion or hobby, like knitting quilts or gluing collages, that's all well and good. Have a good time making that first draft, and move onto the next to keep you occupied. But if your goal is to create products for sale to the film and television industry, expect multiple, almost constant revision passes until the script is sold or optioned. It's during those reviews and edits that you prove your dedication, desire, and worthiness to play in the grown-up Hollywood's game. That's why they call writing "work," and if you don't like hard work, go sell shoes.

Revision Soapbox

When I was earning my Master of Fine Arts in Screenwriting from Loyola Marymount University in Los Angeles, I knew some very talented young writers. A couple won major national awards and screenwriting contests when they were still students. They interned at production companies as writer's assistants and story editors. They earned the attention of agents and managers, and a long, profitable career as a writer seemed to lay itself out before them. One of those writers is now a production accountant, and the other is selling medical supplies in Austin, TX. What happened? They reveled in the creative orgasm of the first draft, the grand illusion of "flow" as completed pages piled up and scenes seemed to write themselves. The natural buzz of banging nouns and verbs together into an entity that seemed more like a living, breathing thing than a mere story was addictive... but the critical notes and unavoidable revision phase was the "comedown." Those withdrawal symptoms were so unpleasant that they let their talent and passion whither away. Now, whatever beautiful, important works they might have once created will never be, and I see a sad, unnecessary waste in that.

Moreover, I never understood why the editing phase was a shock to their (or any other writer's) systems. Perhaps they sought perfection in the first draft, but did they honestly think that was achievable? Did they think that the demand for hard work, commitment, and thoroughness didn't apply to the arts? When you consider how competitive the creative fields are because of the sheer amount of people wishing to break into them, the need to pore over your work until it's the absolute best it can be becomes even more important.

Ironically, even amidst all this rigorous attention to details, screenwriters don't have the demand for immediate perfection that other professions face. In other professions, from professional athlete to accountancy, mistakes are not tolerated. The pro must get it right the first time. If a surgeon loses his or her patient on the operating table because of an unkind cut, the doctor can't call a "do-over." If a basketball player misses a potentially game-winning free throw with :01 left in a Final Four contest, he can't ask for "one more try." Screenwriters catch a break in this department. While screenwriting is just as demanding and competitive as any other profession on Earth, movie and TV wordsmiths get to make initial mistakes. If they fail to get their stories straight the first time through, they have the opportunity (and responsibility) to repair the mishaps before anyone else sees the fruits of their labor.

So, if we start at the simplest understanding of all this, good writing is rewriting. It's perhaps the most utilized cliché of all for professional wordsmiths. However, no cliché rings with more truth. How well a screenwriter revises his or her own work will greatly determine how well a story is told. More importantly, the revision drafts determine how the screenplay is received by producers, executives, actors, and agents. Every scriptwriter worth his or her weight in brass fasteners knows that the first draft does not make the script. The first go around can produce inspired images, sensitive characters, and entertaining plot twists. Odds are, though, it will also produce wordy dialogue, flabby description, and a handful of spelling errors and assorted typos. Now the real work starts. Unfortunately, screenwriters aren't reporters or nonfiction book authors who have copyeditors to catch mistakes. (I intentionally type extra errors into my manuscripts to give my editors something to do — like inserting the wrong banana in a sentence.) The screenwriter must perform revisions "alone in a room."

It's a chore. That's why amateur writers don't utilize this creative stage as well as professionals. While three hours can pass like ten minutes when a writer is really rolling, those same three hours can pass like three days. Every distraction calls a little louder. When it's time to revise, a screenwriter will take a longer lunch or hear the call of every bad TV show.

I overcome the revision woes with a few simple practices. First, I consider that every minute I spend revising my work is another minute that's separating me from the competition. If you ever stepped foot in any agency or studio script reader's room or storage vault, you'll be blown away by the seemingly infinite volume of scripts lining the walls. Imagine the warehouse scene from *Raiders of the Lost Ark*. It's like that. It's all too easy for your script to vanish into those depths forever if you give readers reason to bury it due to lack of revision. So I consider the following creative equation...

$(R)evision = (C)ompetition \div 2$:
So, if 1,000 of your competing writers start writing screenplays, only half will ever have the fortitude to finish them. So you just cut your odds in half if you wrap up that first draft. Of the remaining 500 between you and a sale, half of those won't revise their script. So tackle that page-one rewrite, and you're running with 250 bulls now. Every revision pass you make is one additional step the other losers can't manage, and you cut that pool down another 50% until it's just you and a six figure check.

Keep that in mind, and it might help kick you in the behind when you really don't want to tackle another edit. In the end, it's all about desire and discipline.

To keep me on that discipline track moving ever forward, I write the first draft all the way through from start to finish — never stopping in midstream to fix a section I know was imperfect. Every first draft is imperfect. It's the sketch you pencil on a canvas before laying on the completed oil painting through hours of work later in the process. However, if you get into the habit of constantly writing and then rewriting what you just wrote until those few pages are "perfect," you'll become trapped in that "one step forward, two steps back cycle" that creates the endless pile of unfinished scripts. You don't need to write from start to finish. If the ending is clearer in your mind than the third act, begin there — but as soon as that's in the can, get on with other scenes. Keep moving forward. That's a very serious suggestion because I've seen talented writers and directors collapse because of their inability to allow imperfection and move on in their work. I had a friend from my film school days who planned, wrote, and started some outstanding projects. He had a truly refined and subtle artistic sense, and I'm sure he would have created outstanding movies — first as independent films and later for the studios. But he was perpetually insecure and unhappy about his work because he couldn't get it precisely as he conceived it. To his mind, it wasn't perfect, so it shouldn't have existed. I suppose I'm glad that principle doesn't apply to people.

I was very fortunate in my education and preparation because I was first trained as a reporter. I worked for newspapers and magazines before I began screenwriting. That work in journalism taught me to write on deadline. I had to get all of my stories in on time and get them into the best shape I could possibly manage in the time allowed. Perfect or not, when the deadline hit, I had to hand it in and move on to the next. And, perhaps that's the best and most succinct advice I can give to any writer..."On to the next. Always on to the next."

Return of the Reeves-Stevens...es...

Remember Judith and Garfield Reeves-Stevens? Well, they're back, and they agree with my straight-ahead philosophy. Since they are constantly working on major projects for the big studios, and they've published more novels than I've had severe migraines, they must juggle all of those projects by paying rigorous attention to procedure and detail and to clearly divide creative stages between writing and revising. The team might be micro-managing multiple drafts of several television episodes while polishing a 300- to 400-page novel manuscript. The publishers or producers paying for that material care little how much other work is on the desk of a writer. They want their finished product on time, every time.

Both writers agreed that it's best for writers to follow their lead and push through the first draft, regardless of quality: "Avoid going through everything you've already written each day and looking for areas to polish before you move on because you risk becoming trapped in a cycle of constantly working backward and never finishing anything," Judith said. "You need to maintain your momentum, and there is time later for rewriting."

"That said, I do read the previous day's work before I start writing every morning," Garfield admitted. "But I do that only to get the flow of where I was in the story when I quit the previous day. If I do spot anything that I'm not happy with from the previous day, I'll flag it. But I won't go back and rewrite it. I move forward to the page goal set for that day. Every professional writer reaches that point in their manuscript in which they switch from writer to editor. Half of writing is rewriting, and that's when you go over everything you've produced and begin editing what you've already done."

"Our work goes through three stages before it goes to the editor or producer," Judith said. "One of us writes an original draft — as much as we intended to complete for that day. Then, the other looks over that work, making notes, suggestions, et cetera. Finally, we both review all of the changes and form the draft for submission. Nothing leaves the office for outside eyes until we sign off on every word. To keep track of such a complicated process, we print out all of our work with the initials of whomever last reviewed it along with time code down to the second. That way, we're always sure that whatever draft we're looking at is the correct one with the most updated material."

However, once a writer pushes through the long first draft stage and must now begin editing his or her work, how does that scribe know what stays and what dies bathed in red ink?

"Much of that is instinct," Garfield said. "A sense of when your story is working, or what's preventing it from coming together. That instinct comes from reading and watching stories. Reading novels. Watching movies. Watching your favorite television shows. You develop the ability to feel what works for a story and why. That gives you the ability to cut a scene or an element that you love, but that you know simply doesn't work or doesn't fit. It's difficult, but you can always save what you cut and perhaps use it in another story down the line. It's that old cliché that being a writer means reading and writing every day. But that shouldn't be difficult. You're a writer. That's what you do, and it's how you develop your skills."

Do What I Do... Maybe.

In my own work, once I finish that first draft, I make it easier on myself to edit and revise by sticking to the same routine on every project. First, I read the script aloud, paying attention to what I hear — not just reciting. You catch such a variety of potential errors through this very simple step. If you read silently, your eyes can gloss over an error because your mind knows what you *meant* to write or how it *should* sound. Reading aloud causes your eyes and comprehensive faculties to take just that split-second delay as your mouth forms and utters the words. It's hard for anything to get past your editorial eye that way. Also, this verbal read-through can give you a sense of pacing in both dialogue and structure. Obviously, if you get bored reading it, so will a producer or script reader. Once this initial polish is complete, it's up to you whether you submit your first draft for reactions and notes.

After I go through the notes phase and compile all of the opinions I value, I decide whether or not the script needs fine-tuning or a page-one rewrite. If all indications tell me that I need a sizable overhaul, I start from page one and rewrite the script. The script invariably turns out better — paced more smoothly and filled with better dialogue because I'm no longer worrying about where the story might go. I might keep an element that I really like or that clearly worked, but I'll come up with entirely new material to tell the story. Too many inexperienced writers try to cheat the page one rewrite and just fix sections of the script — like sweeping dust under a throw rug and vacuuming around it. If the script isn't working as a unified unit, fixing parts of it will not only fail to fix the script, it can turn it into such an abhorrent mess that nothing but a total "start from scratch" can save it.

Too Many Cooks

Steven E. de Souza knows the value of a page one rewrite. Sure, this A-List action writer gets paid for every draft, but he knows there's no substitution for a true revision for creating an effective script. He began his career in television as a writer, director and producer on such shows as *Knight Rider*, *V*, *Tales from the Crypt*, and the animated *Cadillacs and Dinosaurs*. His feature career took off in the 1980s with credits including *48 Hours*, *Die Hard*, *Commando*, and *The Running Man*. He has become one of Hollywood's top action writers. His other credits include writer and director on *Streetfighter* and co-credit on *The Flintstones*.

De Souza said he usually completes a script before beginning revision. He may begin with the beginning or end; or he may write specific action sequences he envisions for the story and flesh out the entire tale using those scenes as a framework.

He writes with a personal computer both during the first draft and rewrite stage. However, he edits his work on paper with the aid of a writer's assistant. An aspiring screenwriter may not be able to afford an assistant, but the editing and revision process work the same with or without an extra set of hands to handle the pages. When finished with a draft, de Souza will print out the entire script and edit line by line with a red pen. While he still looks for any typos, stray grammatical errors, or odd spelling mistakes that the word processor program didn't catch, de Souza uses the editing time to eliminate every unnecessary sequence, paragraph, sentence, or word.

Appropriate to his reputation as an action master, he refers to the process as making the script "bulletproof": "No one should ever submit a first draft. You should submit a fourth or fifth draft and call it your first. That means writing the script through several times — not fixing bits and pieces of it. That's like pulling the threads on a sweater."

De Souza used words like "wordy" and "flabby" when describing the work of many young writers. He was quick to point out that a screenwriter with genuine talent can sabotage himself or herself by not being ruthless enough on his or her own work. He stressed that too many writers take a soft attitude when presenting their work — hoping the story catches a reader's eye as a product and not as entertainment on the written page.

"You have to realize that the reader is your first audience," de Souza said. "You have to entertain the reader first before it goes any further."

Finally, a big part of knowing your how to revise your work is hampered by ego. It's a writer's cliché that you must "eat your babies," but that serves to explain how you need to separate yourself from the work during revision. If writers are so defensive that they believe that first draft is the Bible, they're putting up defenses to protect their ego. A lot of a writer's self-worth is tied up in the work, and when that work is attacked, it can feel personal — even if the attack is honestly intended to make the work better.

I learned to use that natural defensive mechanism to my advantage. When my work is criticized, and you can be sure I get the same amount of positive and negative input as you do, I try to sense exactly how upset that inner artistic voice of mine gets. However, while some writers might steer clear or avoid criticism that annoys them, I latch onto it. The more irritated I feel, the more I believe the criticism is justified because I can't believe that I missed whatever error I made. Also, a good note means more long hours of revision, and no writer really enjoys that. That's when I need to bow my neck and grind out the new pages.

Larry DiTillio believes that this sensitive and defensive reputation of writers in Hollywood can often work against them. He specializes in writing science fiction, fantasy, and children's animation for television. Currently the head writer on the children's action cartoon *Beast Wars*, DiTillio has most recently served as story editor and writer for the science fiction series *Babylon 5*. He has written for sci-fi and animated series on multiple networks.

"One of the problems writers have is that they can be their own worst enemies. They can get a reputation as a loose cannon very easily when it comes time to revise their work according to what a producer or executive says. They resist or resent the notes they get."

When writing for television, you will probably want to avoid long lists of nitpicky notes from TV executives. To keep your TV script as free from such outside influence as possible, DiTillio urges you to get your work in the best shape possible before submitting it up the line. He added that TV writers can often face very tight rewrite deadlines, much more severe than those a feature film writer might face. So a TV scribe not only has to face input from multiple non-writing sources, he or she has to implement that input in a very short time.

"The best way to avoid that situation is to turn in the first draft that's mainly all there," he added.

Again, DiTillio put the responsibility of revising solely on the writer's back. If he or she can soundly construct their script on their own desks, it'll pass the desks of others much faster and much easier.

"The key to all this is not just knocking off a first draft quickly and turning it in. It's spending time with the first draft and rewriting it four or five times before you hand it in and call it a first draft. That way you cut way down on your rewrite time."

DiTillio uses this technique to ensure that, when he finishes a teleplay, he knows it's all there. "When I turn in a script, I know the structure is right. I know just from reading it that the pacing is right. I can read the script on my own and know that the pace is not right. Then I can go in there and start cutting away. Maybe the story beats are in the wrong places. Maybe the dialogue is too wordy. Whatever the problems might be, my revision make certain that I catch and fix them on my time before anyone else reads the end product. By spending so much time on the beginning of a project, I needn't worry so much about subsequent drafts beyond a few line changes here and there."

Finally, DiTillio urged aspiring TV writers to really analyze their story ideas and outlines before they even begin writing. This way a writer can see areas where the plot might slow down or simply not work at all. By looking for the areas that offer story problems before they're even written, a screenwriter would save the time of needing to cut or rewrite those sections later.

Hopefully, you're getting the message that the eventual responsibility for the quality of your work throughout the revision process rests solely with you. Whether you're working alone on a project close to your heart or putting together a story for another entity, that script goes out into the world to represent you — your talent, your professional commitment, and your future intentions as a writer. So, why wouldn't you want to slave over that script until it shows you at your best?

That's a question Richard Krevolin puts to his students constantly. A professor at the USC Film School, this playwright, screenwriter, poet, and author holds a BA from Yale and Master's Degree in Screenwriting from UCLA. He also completed a Master's in playwriting and fiction from USC before teaching for the institution.

When you ask him what he teaches his students — young men and women learning the craft and struggles of good film and television writing just as you are — Krevolin comes right out and says what a professional screenwriter must be prepared to do in Hollywood: "The joke about the process of revision for a screenwriter is that he or she will revise whatever the studio says to revise as long as he or she gets paid. While that is part of the business, the truth is a little more artistic than that."

However, as an aspiring pro, you're not rewriting to be paid by the draft. You're putting in your effort to compile the finest script you can to make that first sale, to earn that first assignment, or to draw attention to your talent. Krevolin repeatedly stressed that a screenwriter like you must have the ability to face and evaluate himself or herself and admit that not every word set on the page is perfect.

"There comes that moment when you have to admit it's not perfect, and that's hard to do. You might get angry, or you might think the person criticizing the work is an idiot... but eventually, you realize that the criticism is right. Then you have to get back in there and revise. Just as mothers are reluctant to let go of their children, so writers can be reluctant to let go of their favorite scene or to make changes.

"I think all projects have a certain point where you have to let go, but a writer needs to develop that sense of when it's time to complete this project and move on to the next one. You're going to release it to an actor or a director to interpret your script anyway, so making the script as good as it can possibly be only serves to increase your control over the product. They'll be less likely to change a good piece of art significantly. You have control over the project before it reaches those stages. You can shape the story into an original vision before anyone else gets to it — if you are self-critical and can admit shortcomings in the work."

Personally, I recommend that, if you're not struggling through a page-one rewrite, you consider every rewrite a focal point for an individual problem area within a script. Perhaps one rewrite deals only with a certain character's development. Maybe the next focuses on dialogue... the next on plotting. By tackling problems one at a time, a screenwriter can remain much more focused on the story as a whole and avoid getting intimidated or overwhelmed by the rewrite process.

"If writers thought beforehand of all the revisions they'd need to do to complete a project," Krevolin joked, "we'd be crippled before we started."

He offers a list of useful checkpoints a script should pass before it leaves the writer's hands. Each checkpoint on this list could be the focus of a revision draft. Consider this list of ten examples:

1. Never have two characters agree on anything. Did you release the tension from your tires before you got off the road?
2. Don't split your heavy into two or more people. A good heavy = a good heavy.
3. Have at least one strong, castable leading role.
4. Have I ever seen anything before? Always be original and full of surprises.
5. End with one final. Not four quarterfinals.

6. In every scene, come in late and get out early.

7. Every scene must end in a different place than it began.

8. Your main character must have arc/growth/epiphany.

9. In dialogue, brevity is the filet of soul.

10. With your characters, did you scab the wound?

These points could change from script to script or writer to writer. However, the spirit behind them remains the same. A writer needs to examine their script on level after level, scene-by-scene, word after word. He or she needs to have the script in the best possible shape imaginable because screenwriters tend to lose control of their work once it ventures into the marketplace.

So, in the end, you have as much freedom of choice during the revision process as you do when choosing your genre, subject matter, et cetera. There is no proverbial gun to your head forcing you to revise your work. You decide if your story calls for revision, how much is necessary, how many times you wish to revise, et cetera. But while perfection is impossible to obtain, you need to ask yourself how close to perfection you're willing to come. Forget the script as a stack of paper telling a story. Are you and your ambitions worth the hours required to make your work as good as it can possibly be. Only you can answer that, and only you can do the work. As a screenwriter, you must master the craft with hard work and attention to detail, even if it means admitting you're simply not the world's greatest writer... yet.

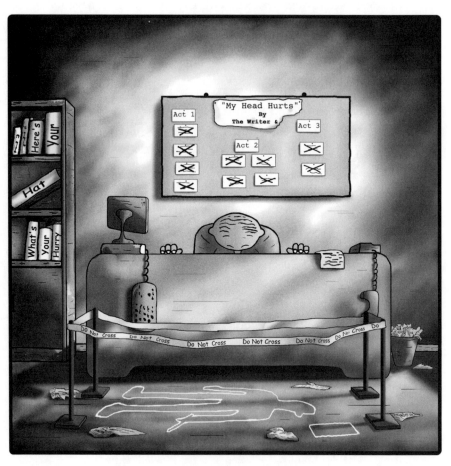

Sadly, some partnerships just don't work out.

chapter five

Writing Comedy:
Make 'em Laugh or Else

You probably heard this little pearl of wisdom before, but writing comedy is high risk/high gain. It's tough — potentially tougher than writing long-form drama. Why? Because you have to be funny. Duh! Right? Well, you have to be funny while composing a narrative that is every bit as airtight and effective as a drama. You just added a whole new universe of troubles to your screenwriting — already the most difficult, disciplined written art form ever conceived by humankind.

Just to brighten your day a little more, the effectiveness of your comedy writing is entirely subjective. Whether or not someone laughs at a joke is based almost entirely on the personality and sense of humor of the reader. There're some ways to skirt the problem — such as writing something that's a little more lowbrow, common denominator humor. In other words, you can go for the cheap, easy laughs. Fortunately, there's a place for that in the marketplace. Just look at *There's Something about Mary, American Pie,* or *Dumb and Dumber.* They were all successful, but none of them could exactly split the atom. In fact, you could argue that the only intelligent comedies coming out these days are inbound from the UK. From *A Fish Called Wanda* to *About a Boy,* they've more or less had that market cornered.

However, even if you reach out for the fart joke crowd, you're still a potential victim of that "is it funny?" curse. You'd be amazed how fast the wind can change about what's funny. It almost seems like the comedy fashions shift with the seasons as if some runway in Paris comes up with them. I optioned a comedy to an L.A. director amidst multiple offers on what everyone thought was a sure-fire, high-concept pitch. That guy couldn't get his stuff together. When that option ended, I polished up the script for another go at the marketplace. I was all ready for another beeline to my script because it had been such a hot property just six months before. But... nothing. Crickets chirping. Tumbleweeds rolling by my door. Zip. So, just in that six-month period, the comedy winds changed for me.

When you approach comedy writing you might get the "Can you be funny?" question. When I once told my manager (bless his heart) that I wanted to write a spec comedy next, he asked me, "Well, are you funny?" What do you say to that? "No, actually I'm a witless load who's never brought a smile to the face of a single human being — except for one baby this one time (but that was just gas)." Obviously, it helps to write comedy if you have a strong sense of humor, but the trick is getting that wit down on the page while telling your story. Hopefully, you can begin with confidence in your sense of humor and invest yourself in developing an effective comic narrative.

How do you that? I only have about 55,000 words here, and there are endless volumes out there dealing specifically with the art form of writing comedy. However, off the cuff, I would recommend any aspiring comedy writer start with Aristotle's *Poetics*. No other work is as effective on presenting the essentials of creating the comic hero. And if you have your protagonist down solid, you're that much closer to getting the script out there.

For more insights into the inner workings of writing comedy for film and television, we again turn to working professionals. The input below comes exclusively from writers making their living making people laugh while telling stories. You'll come away with a glimpse into their creative philosophies and their work experiences.

Larry Gelbart: Comedy Legend

It's not often you get the opportunity to interview a legend. And it's extraordinary when you have a chance to learn from him. Fortunately, I had the first experience, and you're about to enjoy the second.

Larry Gelbart's bio and resume is so extensive that, if I included every word, it could literally chew up almost 5% of my target word count for this book. His writing, producing, and directing career extends from the age of radio to the present — making him one of the great comedy minds of the twentieth century.

Obviously, he's probably best known as one of the powerful forces behind the classic sitcom *M*A*S*H* — one of the true touchstones of the medium. But he began his career in 1946 writing for Danny Thomas and the *Maxwell Coffee Time* show. He went on to write for Eddie Cantor, Bob Hope and Jack Paar.

Moving to television once that medium took over, Gelbart wrote for *The Bob Hope Show*, *The Red Buttons Show*, *The Pat Boone Show*, *The Art Carney Specials*, *The Danny Kaye Show*, *The Marty Feldman Comedy Machine*, and, of course, *M*A*S*H*. He also managed to fit in writing for the Oscar broadcasts in 1985 and 1986.

His film credits include *Mastergate*, *Barbarians at the Gate*, *Weapons of Mass Distraction*, *And Starring Pancho Villa as Himself*, *Oh, God!*

(screenplay nominated for Academy Award), *Tootsie*, (screenplay nominated for Academy Award), *Blame it on Rio*, and the remake of *Bedazzled*.

A renowned playwright, his credits include classics like *A Funny Thing Happened on the Way to the Forum*, *City of Angels*, and *Peter and the Wolf* for the American Ballet Theatre.

His awards could fill the wing of a museum, including the Tony for *A Funny Thing Happened on the Way to the Forum* and *City of Angels*, the Emmy for *M*A*S*H* and *Barbarians at the Gate*, and the Writers Guild of America Award for Writing for *Oh, God!*, *Tootsie*, *M*A*S*H*, and *Barbarians at the Gate*. He also took home the Writers Guild of America Lifetime of Career Excellence Tribute, the Humanitas Award, the Peabody Award, the Edgar Allan Poe Award, the New York Film Critics' Award, National Society of Film Critics' Award, the Lee Strasberg Award for Lifetime Achievement in the Arts and Sciences, and the Cable Ace Award. You'll also find him inducted in the California Broadcasters Association Hall of Fame and the Theater Hall of Fame.

Convinced he might have something useful to say about the art and inner workings of comedy writing? Good... because I asked him, since he had the advantage of having been a working professional in the industry for many years, how has the writing business changed as he watched it evolve from the inside?

"Writers today receive far more payment than they've ever before enjoyed," Gelbart said. "And — for more abuse. From executives, from directors, from stars. The only constant is the indifference the public has as to who wrote what."

Contrary to popular belief, Gelbart denies that writing comedy is somehow more challenging than writing drama. "Writing comedy is only difficult for those who have no reason to believe that they can — and very often don't have a clue that they shouldn't be attempting it. The same is true of those who write (or try) more dramatic material."

Since he was one of the driving forces behind what many say is the greatest sitcom of all time, what does he think of the current state of sitcoms? A lot of people in the business believe they are in decline. Does he agree?

"I am not all that familiar with the quality of situation comedies today. They were never my favorite form of viewing. I must confess that I never saw an episode of *Lucy* — or a *Bilko*. That was not a judgment on the shows, but rather the form."

So it's safe to say he saw an episode of *M*A*S*H*, but for Gelbart, writing sitcoms was another comedy writing gig. "Of course, there have been excellent sitcoms, and ones that are beneath the bottom of the barrel. That was always true. It must be especially difficult to maintain the quality of modern-day half-hours, which aren't half-hours at all. Most have only twenty-two minutes of content, and some are closer to twenty-one. It is impossible to tell a good story, people it with good characters, and have the process interrupted up to nineteen times by commercials and promotional material. And then, add the crowning insult of making the names of those who were responsible for the show all but illegible, so that more network executives or show hyping can take center screen."

While Gelbart was writing for television sitcom comedy, he had to produce fresh material in every episode for familiar faces. Did he deliberately keep in mind the actors for whom he was writing — or does he write for the characters and trust the actors to work themselves into the material?

"When you're writing comedy for recurring characters, you quite naturally fashion your material for those actors who play their roles. Should you introduce a new character, an original, you write what you have in mind, then cast the actor to match what — and who — you had in mind. Quite possibly, once that actor is hired, you might make some adjustments in your writing to maximize the qualities that actor brings to the part. In writing a spec movie script, it's best not to have any specific actors in mind. Chances are very low that you'll be that lucky."

I would add that you should never add new characters into a show formula if you are writing a spec episode of any particular show as a writing sample. You need to show that you can write for the characters and the show model already in use. You can't presume that you know the show better than those who created it and cast it do. So show that you can write specifically for what they already have in place.

If you can write that golden spec — if you can in fact write funny material — can you write your own ticket in Hollywood? Or are there always other factors in play?

"Being able to write in a truly humorous way will open many a door for you in this business. It takes other factors, as well. You have to be smart, you have to pick the right people to work with — or be lucky enough to be hired by them. You need good representation. You need good advice. You have to listen to others. Take what's good and use it. Discard the rest. And marry a friend."

I doubt that last bit of advice is useful only for comedy writers. Still, what does he think is the hardest truth that writers need to come to terms with if they want to work in this business?

"The strongest temptation in this town is to rewrite even the best writer. If you give in to this madness, you may wind up with a Porsche SUV in your garage, but an unmistakable empty space in your soul."

Well, he got all spiritual on me there — and I have nothing to add to that. So, before you realize how shallow I am, we move on for comedic insights from other professionals working in the business.

Mike Bender

Lost in the advertising and marketing world of bustling Manhattan, Mike Bender made a career change, and he hasn't looked back since. A writer on *Not Another Teen Movie* and the Halloween comedy, *A Fistful of Candy*, Bender is on his way to a successful career in screenwriting.

"I started working at New Line as a marketing intern in New York," Bender said. "I did not like marketing, and I started writing. I took the opportunity of being at New Line to write and use their resources. I hoped that, if I wrote something of value, I could get it to go somewhere."

Bender wrote *Gigantic* — a parody of the immensely popular *Titanic* — and sold it to New Line while he was working there. During preproduction on that movie, he worked in L.A. He decided to stay in L.A. and give screenwriting a shot. Off his work on *Gigantic* and his evident skill at parody, Bender got a job writing skits for the MTV Movie Awards. "They were looking for writers to parody short films with Ben Stiller, and I did a spoof of *Mission: Impossible* for them." Off that parody work, Bender got the writing assignment on *Not Another Teen Movie*. Following that film's success, Bender was able to write and pitch his own comedy, *A Fistful of Candy*.

"I realized there's never really been a Halloween kid's comedy. This movie is aimed at a younger audience, but I hope, like *A Christmas Story*, it can attract an adult audience also. There's enough nostalgia in the story to draw in an older following. It's based on the classic western, *Shane*, and its classic themes of redemption. But I'm drawn to comedy — comedies that have heart. But story is the most important aspect of a movie, and a lot of comedies overlook that. We tried to do that with *Not Another Teen Movie*, but some audiences are just looking for a lot of jokes and not as much story. So that film headed in that direction."

Now that Bender has a successful writing assignment and an original spec sale under his belt, he's had to head out into the market to pitch his own stories.

"A pitch is a challenge, because it's tricky. You might think you have it all worked out, but you never know how it's all going to come together until you sit down and try to write it. I have other ideas that I think about, but when you're on a go-project, obviously that takes all of your time.

"Right now, I'm really excited to finish the script for *Fistful of Candy* because it's an original concept. The problem with writing a parody that was successful like *Not Another Teen Movie* was that I got a lot of parodies thrown at me as potential jobs. So it was good to pitch and get my own idea out there to avoid getting pigeon-holed as a parody writer."

Ironically, I know many of the aspiring scribes out there clutching this thick plain of smashed wood pulp would gladly suffer such pigeonholing if it meant a long and fruitful career. Still, developing comedy writing skills takes time — as much time as building your career. And it also takes a lot of luck, as you're about to learn.

Adam "Tex" Davis

Adam "Tex" Davis took a strange and coincidence-filled path to success in Hollywood. A 1993 graduate of NYU, he followed the lead of many film school graduates and spent the next couple of years working various jobs and finishing his first professional short film. He worked with Todd Phillips, director of the teen comedy *Road Trip*, and the two produced and starred in *Killing Time*, a half-hour short that made the rounds on the festival circuit.

"I played a character named Tex, and Todd played Weasel. The film would either win or fail to get anywhere in the festivals. But managers Craig Perry and Chris Bender of Zide Management saw it and liked it. They called me up and asked if I had any scripts. They got me an agent, and I wrote a film called *Sunburned*. It was a spring break comedy that didn't sell. But MTV saw the script and liked it. They hired me to write a film for them called *Spring Break Lawyer*. Not long after that, Miramax bought *Sunburned*. Finally, New Line bought another script of mine (*Just Friends*), so everything more or less came together fairly quickly for me."

Since that initial run of good luck, Davis earned rewrites on *Ten Wishes* for Fox, a rewrite of a comic strip adaptation (*Zits*) and a rewrite for Universal on the script, *Good and Dead*. Now, Davis is focused on "Gardener of Eden" — a spec script that he'd like to write and direct. Leonardo DiCaprio's company optioned it, and business is moving forward on the project.

"I wrote comedies so far, but I'd like to branch out into different kinds of material. I would like to do a horror film, and I wrote a big fantasy adventure — but *Lord of the Rings* shelved that for a while. I'd love to do something more dramatic, but I don't think I could do a straight drama without a little comedy. I've always been drawn to comedy. I think that interest has to come to you — almost innately. I even tried stand-up for a while, but found it too unnerving. So I decided that I'd just put these jokes into scripts. At first, I had trouble with that because I needed to develop plots to hang them on. My manager was instrumental in getting me to think about the story — getting the jokes to come out of the character and story structure. It was a learning process."

And therein lies a huge secret of comedy writing. You don't compose a list of jokes and find a story or premise to hang them on when you write. You get your premise together first and make sure you develop an airtight story. If that work is done, your jokes and comic scenes must then grow out of that story. If anything is forced into the story just for cheap laughs, it's going to feel out of place. The audience will sense the break in continuity, and your script will suffer.

As for Davis, he looks to write every day at his home in Brooklyn. But he said that doesn't interfere with his ability to do business in the industry: "I go to L.A. for about two or three weeks, two or three times a year. It's tough to pitch over the phone, though I have done that. So I pack my meetings together and do them face to face while in California."

As for writers hoping to reach Davis' level of writing success, he said he refers many people to media publications like the daily trades and other specific screenwriting magazines for inspiration and education. And he reminds them of his favorite quote: "Nothing in the world can take the place of persistence. Nothing is more common than unsuccessful men with talent." Thanks to Calvin Coolidge for that one.

"I saw that quote on a porno website, while I was taking a break," Davis said. "It shows you that inspiration can hit you anywhere."

Now before we wrap up our look at comedy writing, we're going to cheat a little. A later chapter looks specifically at the challenges set before writing partners who work in comedy. Our next interview subjects could find a home there. After all, they are a writing team, and they do write comedy. But I wanted to include them here because it gives you some insight into the minds of comedy writers who are very hot. I caught up to these guys just as their most recent script was booming at the box office. So, is it possible to be funny — and suddenly wealthy — all at the same time?

Glenn Ficarra and John Requa

Glenn Ficarra and John Requa exploded onto the Hollywood writing scene big time in 2003 with the smash hit, controversial comedy, *Bad Santa*. The film was the lone comedic hit of that year-end Christmas season — partly because it was funny and partly because these writers were able to stir up more than their share of trouble with such a salty holiday movie.

"We met in college — at film school," Requa said. "We wrote short films together and made them together. Eventually, we moved out here together and attended a few festivals. We were starving filmmakers for about seven years until we got a job a Nickelodeon through a friend and started working in animation — on a show called *Angry Beavers*."

The team's short films were mainly sketch comedy pieces — similar to those of the popular comedy team The Kids in the Hall. Both writers called their short comic pieces "a little twisted." But they always included an emphasis on cinematic form. For all intents and purposes, they were mini cinematic comedy action sequences.

"We're filmmakers first and writers second," Ficarra said. "It helps to know the practicalities of writing going into production. Our short films were all short set pieces, so we became adept at writing set pieces and turning them into overall movies. In general, any experience we've had in film, visual effects, or in an art department trained us for our movies."

In fact, Requa and Ficarra's experience is important to note for aspiring Hollywood writers. It's not enough for you to pay your dues in Hollywood as writers. You have to pay them as just working professionals. I was a writing assistant, a bodyguard, a house sitter, a dog walker, a house painter, a construction worker, a self-defense teacher, a PR writer, and a hen teaser. Since any experience you gain prepares you as a writer, that's all positive. But any entry-level writer should prepare him or herself for a variety of chaotic piecework jobs.

Requa and Ficarra built sets, edited, worked as a visual effects rigger, served as an optical printer, and toiled as a telemarketer. Their jobs ran the gamut, including periods working at the same commercial and music video production companies.

Along the way, they came up with two feature screenplays, *Jack Tucker* and *47 Dead Bodies* — two popular reads that jumpstarted their screenwriting careers. "Eventually, they all got optioned at one time or another. Now, Jack Tucker will go into production in April 2004. We're directing with Woody Harrelson starring. It's a comedy road movie like *Pee Wee's Big Adventure* — as done maybe by the Coen brothers."

However, their first hit was *Cats and Dogs*, the summer comedy that got them noticed and their current offices on the Warner Bros. lot.

"To get the writing done, we have desks that face each other," Requa said. "We have one computer with two monitors and two keyboards. We never write away from each other. Not a word is written separately. And as long as we're funny, we want to keep writing comedies. I think we're comfortable writing them. Even if we were to write a drama, it would have comedic elements. But we do love genre movies. We wrote a zombie movie and have pitches for blaxploitation films, et cetera. But they still had funny moments."

As for *Bad Santa*, the Coen brothers wanted to hire writers for films they could produce or executive produce aside from the films that the pair write and direct themselves.

Ficarra explained, "We had dinner with them. They had a pitch for a movie called *Bad Santa*. It was, 'He drinks beer and stuff.' We wanted to do a comedy heist movie using a department store Santa and elf helper who rob a store blind on Christmas. But they encounter a kid who thinks he's really Santa. Circumstances dictate that Santa ends up at the kid's house. From there, it's a sociopath living with a kid."

"The Coens liked it. We did a couple of drafts, and they offered very tight, laser beam notes. They're writers, too. So, you're getting notes from a writer — great notes that were well focused and very helpful toward getting the script done. It was a pleasure to work with them."

In the future, Requa and Ficcara hope to build on their experience of working with the Coen brothers. They now seem on course to becoming two of the biggest comedy writers in the business — and, perhaps, competition for the Coens themselves.

Now, we'll return to comedy writing in a few pages when we examine comedy writing teams. However, for now we'll ride the writing team momentum that Glenn Ficarra and John Requa provided and turn our attention to the strange word of successful writing partnerships.

section two

The Writing Team

While using his powers of dramatic invention,
The Writer gets caught in a tangled web of intrigue.

chapter six

Verbal Alchemy:
Managing the Writing Team

A successful Hollywood writing team is a rare gestalt creature — a force of creativity stronger than the sum of its parts that seems to come into existence entirely on its own. These powerful partnerships can't be artificially forged as the recipe for a writing team is too delicate a recipe to mass-produce. The team requires equal parts talent, trust, respect, ego, humility, organization, delegation, tolerance, and that rarest of all elements — chemistry. You could no more "arrange" a successful writing team than you could force together a happy shotgun marriage. It's almost as if the two halves that make the screenwriting whole must find each other for the system to work.

I have always admired good writing teams. They fascinate me because I was never able to work as part of one. I wrote for television as part of a staff, collaborating to create comedy sketches with a large group of writers. I remember that experience fondly as we kicked ideas back and forth. The litmus test for a joke was whether you cracked up the guys around the bullpen. We ended up putting in sixteen-hour days, but the hours flew by with constant laughter. The worst part of the workday wasn't getting out of bed; it was heading home after the chuckling died down.

However, even after that positive creative experience, I never worked with a single partner that seemed to click with me creatively. Maybe I was a better writer than he was, and I was dragging him along. Maybe she was sharper than me on the page and wanted to move out on her own. Maybe the other guy lost passion for an individual project and gave up before it was done. I either worked too fast or not thoroughly enough. I liked action, and she enjoyed dialogue. Regardless of the reason, I always end up writing alone.

One more time...

So I long to know what makes a good writing team work. Where does the creativity flow from when two people settle down before the keyboard? Does one team member write, while the other edits? How does a team settle a difference of opinion? To answer these questions, I sat down with some of the top writing teams in Hollywood. And just so you're immediately comfortable with the writing team concept, I want to revisit the Reeves-Stevens one last time because they are the absolute rarest of Hollywood writing tandems — the successful husband-and-wife team. When you consider that many couples believe it's dangerous for a marriage for spouses to work together, it's amazing that the pair not only enjoys working together — but it seems to cement their personal relationship in productivity and contentment.

"We get along as well as writers as we do as husband and wife," Garfield said.

But, Judith added, "With the exception that Garfield is very sloppy, and I am very neat. My work space is always very organized, but if anything goes into Gar's office, it's never coming out."

The pair met while working at the same educational publishing house in Canada. Garfield was a promotional copywriter and author, while Judith worked as an editor and proofreader. Cupid's arrow struck home while they were working on the same projects, and a successful writing career grew from that powerful personal and professional partnership. Their relationship survived the transition from publishing employees to independent authors — and the move from Toronto to California.

It's easy to see how these two work so well together as even their answers to my questions seemed in sync. They don't so much finish each other's thoughts, but complete them — adding a little bit here and there to round out the concept to its fullest possible understanding. I imagine that's very much how they write.

"I was writing horror novels originally, though we both had an interest in science fiction," Garfield said.

Judith added, "Since we worked together well in the publishing office, our creative partnership developed naturally. Our first project together was the *Star Trek* novel, *Memory Prime*. At the time, Simon and Schuster was just starting to publish *Star Trek* books, and we made a cold call to find out if it was possible to propose stories."

PocketBooks asked for a writing sample, and the team sent one of Garfield's novels. It impressed the publisher and cleared the way for the tandem to send along some novel outlines. A stream of books and scripts flowed from that original project.

"We write everything as a team now," Garfield said. "But, as far as rituals go, there's really no difference in how we wrote alone compared to how we write now. The same professional habits go into everything we do."

"Our work goes through three stages before it goes to the editor or producer," Judith said. "One of us writes an original draft — as much as we intended to complete for that day. Then the other looks over that work, making notes, suggestions, et cetera. Finally, we both review all of the changes and form the draft for submission. Nothing leaves the office for outside eyes until we sign off on every word. To keep track of such a complicated process, we print out all of our work with the initials of whomever last reviewed it along with time code down to the second. That way, we're always sure that whatever draft we're looking at is the correct one with the most updated material."

In addition to keeping track of every reading of every draft, the tandem is also careful to back-up their data every night — well aware of the common writing horror stories of scribes losing several chapters or entire manuscripts because a hard drive crashed and left no trace of weeks worth of work. They also never change or update their technology during a project. Both prefer Apple computers, and they stick with whatever computer hardware and software they used when they began their latest novel or script to prevent unforeseen bugs or system breakdowns. In fact, computer hardware plays into one of Garfield's rituals. He still uses his old Mac II keyboard. Using a USB/serial port adapter, Garfield manages to keep this relic of the Cold War up and running. The number pad no longer words, so it's a good thing he wasn't born an accountant. However, whether it's a matter of superstition or merely manual comfort, Garfield still writes all of his pages with the several inches-thick, clunky keyboard. If they ever upgrade their desktop machines or laptop computers, the Reeves-Stevens do so only after their latest work is in the hands of the producers or publishers.

Such rigorous attention to procedure and detail is essential when you consider the sheer volume of material the Reeves-Stevens must handle while writing for the motion picture, television, animation, and publishing industries. The team might be juggling multiple drafts of several television episodes while polishing a 300- to 400-page novel manuscript. The publishers or producers paying for that material care little how much other work is on the desk of a writer. They want their finished product on time, every time.

"Regardless of what medium the manuscript is intended for," Garfield explained, "we set a page goal every day. We do nothing else that day until we reach that goal."

"If things are going well, we might push ahead and complete another five or ten pages," Judith said. "But we don't quit for the day until the original goal is met — regardless of the quality of that first draft."

The writing team understands the need to deliver on time because they also sit on the other side of the desk — serving as television producers who managed writing staffs.

"When you're writing on assignment, it is crucial to meet the deadline," Judith said. "This is especially true in television because that works on a very tight schedule. There is a cast and crew waiting for that script, so it must be in on time. If a writer is late on a script, it costs hundreds of thousands of dollars per day."

"A book publisher might be willing to give you an extra couple of days if you give them some advance warning. And feature writers are given less stringent deadlines because they work off by themselves — away from the studio. But if you're on staff or freelancing for a TV show, you must have that work in on time."

Garfield agreed: "As a producer, I can tell you that if you're running a TV show, you'd rather receive a good script on time than a perfect script two days late. If you're late on your deadline, you're costing the producer money. Also, if you're freelancing for a show, you shouldn't worry about producing a perfect script because the show's staff writers are going to rewrite anyway."

Both Judith and Garfield urge aspiring writers not already working on assignment or on-staff to keep themselves motivated by providing themselves with firm, self-imposed deadlines. Essentially, they urge would-be pros to pretend they have a producer or a publisher waiting to receive their manuscript when they're done.

"Those deadlines keep you focused and keep the pages flowing," Judith said. "The habit also prevents you from constantly going back over what you already wrote in the first draft stage. Set a date for you to finish the manuscript, and then set a daily page total. If you miss your goal one day, get back on track the next night. This self-imposed time pressure teaches you discipline and will serve you well when you're writing professionally for an editor or producer."

If a member of the team identifies a problem in the work that results in creative differences, how does the pair settle the dispute — to make sure they never go to bed angry?

"First of all, there never really are disagreements like that because we find that, if one of us has a disagreement with something in the work, it's a result of a problem somewhere else in the story," Garfield explained. "Once we identify where the real problem is and figure out how to fix it, the original problem usually solves itself. Everything falls into place."

Settling such issues as a team helps to keep any tension from leaking from their work into their married life. While other writing teams go home to spouses and pets at the end of a working day, Judith and Garfield must still deal with sick cats, leaking roofs, or gardening snafus after the keys go quiet.

"We keep that separate from the work," Garfield said. "It's important to keep those sort of domestic problems from interfering with getting the pages done every day."

However, it doesn't work the other way as inspiration can sneak in unexpectedly when the pair is out to dinner, driving around Los Angeles, or even while sound asleep. If their muse calls when either spouse is off taking care of more mundane business, he or she simply makes sure to make a note of the idea and present it to the other half during work the next day.

"Other than that, things can get as nasty around here as they might get for a solo writer as deadlines close in and the pressure builds," Judith said. "It's frozen dinners and instant coffee as we work late to get everything done."

Garfield agreed, "No one wants to be around a writer during those last hours of work. I stop shaving, bathing, whatever for a day or two. Hygiene becomes an issue until that manuscript is out the door."

"We've always wanted to have a 'Come as You Are on Deadline' party," Judith added. "We'd invite writers to come as they look right before they finish their work on deadline. It would be wall-to-wall five o'clock shadows, sweats, and bunny slippers."

This author, for one, might like to attend such a party, but I doubt the world is really ready for what I look like as the zero hour approaches and my writer's rituals take their toll. As for the Reeves-Stevens, they always struck me as much too nice to be so successful in Hollywood. So I imagine their well-honed Canadian manners would never allow them to show up at their own party so attired.

Eric Bress and J. Mackye Gruber

It was a strange road that led writing partners Eric Bress and J. Mackye Gruber to each other and to their equally unusual break-in project, *The Butterfly Effect*. The two young men from opposite ends of the country met after college and found enough creative chemistry to weather the rigors of beginning a Hollywood career as a partnership. Gruber searched for the best career path after graduating from USC. He met Bress serving as a soundman on a project outside of school.

"We started writing together then," Gruber said. "It took us about six years before we sold our first project (a TV pilot for ABC). Our first feature script that we sold was entitled *Frozen*. Off of that we got hired to do *Final Destination 2*."

Along the way, the pair also raised money to make an independent film. It made it into the 1998 New York Independent International Film Festival and won Best Comedy.

"It's funny, but it doesn't represent where we've come as writers. We think we've evolved over the years here."

Bress added, "I came out to L.A. from New York in 1993 to show my Dad that I was really serious about trying to make it in this industry."

Following their initial success and independent film efforts, the tandem adapted their style and learned the importance of structure. "It's not necessarily just formula, but the story structure is important in every script," Gruber said. That evolution in their work led to the sale of their passion project, *The Butterfly Effect*. Scheduled for release in early 2004, the film tells the story of a young man struggling to get over harmful memories from his childhood. While doing so, he discovers a technique that allows him to travel back in time and occupy his childhood body — thus changing his history forever. However, he also discovers that every change he makes somehow alters his future. The film stars Ashton Kutcher, Amy Smart, and Eric Stoltz.

"New Line let us direct," Gruber said. "It's everyone's dream to be a director here, but it's so much more important to have a good script to work from when preparing a project."

Though originally comedy writers, the pair found themselves offered many sci-fi projects after *Butterfly Effect*. "We started out as comedy writers, but the first thing we sold was science fiction," Bress said. "And that's Hollywood. They say, 'Oh, they're sci-fi writers.' You get a little pigeonholed, but you have to deal with that. This business is all about persistence and drive. Early on, we had no agent, no manager. But we were out there trying to meet producers. Unfortunately, apparently everyone was a producer. There was no way to get to the real professionals or the studios until our managers got us the meetings and started a career in a really tough industry."

But how does the successful writing/directing team interact?

"Ever since we first started out, we learned that we had to be really disciplined as writers who work together," Gruber said. "Having both of us there in the same room made us disciplined. When we get together, we make sure to put in a full day — from 10 to 7, even when we're writing on spec as opposed to on assignment. We go straight through — taking maybe a half-hour for lunch. But no breaks or video games."

The pair begins by first talking about story. "We put in hours and hours on just the story. Then we go to treatments. Once we have our characters down, we act out the scenes back and forth to each other until we feel we're ready to write it. So it works for us to act off of each other while we're writing."

"We have writer friends who are always talking about their blocks," Gruber said. "I don't want to tell them to get a partner, but it does away with that block because someone else is there to clear the wall. It makes you come up with something because someone else is there working with you. That's especially true for comedy. One of us might wait for the other to turn away from the screen — then type a line. You wait for the other guy to look back. If he laughs, it stays. If not, he erases it."

The tag-team approach also works for sci-fi and action scripts. "We try to impress each other — to be more and more creative," Gruber explained. "Between the two of us, we have seen so many movies. Our combined knowledge of cinema is extensive. So if we come up with something familiar, we know it's already been done and we call it. We can censor and filter each other just to make sure it stays fresh."

Their next film, a big budget, tent-pole movie entitled *Cellular* (to be directed by David Ellis) will remain in the action realm, but there are always elements of humor in their work. "That humor got us in trouble with the first draft of *Final Destination 2* — as we had too much comedy in it," Bress said. "Eventually, people reacted to *Final Destination 2* and said they really liked the humor elements in it."

After *Cellular*, the pair wants to return to comedy and direct their work.

"People have been offering us projects to direct," Gruber said. "But all of them seem familiar — like watered-down projects that could have been great. I think the only way to get something truly special for us is to do it ourselves — something that's a passion to us. The writers trying to write things for us are writing too close to that formula. It'll kill us if we come out with our next project that's sub par. It makes our standards really high. There've been a ton of really solid scripts, but nothing that really hit us hard."

Bress agreed, "You must really love your project because you're going to eat, sleep and breathe it for the next year — or more. With *Butterfly Effect*, what gave it strength is that we worked on it for six years. So many different incarnations and directions developed over that time.

But we ended up knowing so much about those characters that we knew every back-story for every character. It helped to make characters so rich that the actors know who they are."

And the team's upcoming spec comedy promises that same level of fermentation as they've been developing it back and forth for the past year: "After how intense *Butterfly Effect* was," Gruber said, "we just want to laugh again."

And after that look into writing teams, you might want to laugh again, too. So, we're taking a look at comedy writing teams next. Isn't that an amazing transition? Sometimes I amaze myself. Do you see how that dovetails from the last quote there? No? Well, nobody hits it out of the park every time. (Maybe I need a writing partner.)

CAUTION:
Alternate reality under construction.

chapter seven

Make the Other Guy Laugh:
The Comedy Tandem

From my experience, the comedy writing team has one major advantage over the solitary writer. Put simply, the team member always has his or her partner sitting right there to react to a gag or a premise. You have the inestimable value of an immediate gut reaction from another human being. If you make yourself laugh while writing, you're probably onto something funny — but you have to deal with the gnawing doubt that it's a joke only you get. What if your sense of humor is too quirky or out of style? If you go to the movies often, you're probably on the right page and in tune with the comedy marketplace. Still, you can never be 100% sure. If you make the other guy laugh right there on the spot as you're banging away at the keyboard, you know you're that much closer to striking gold.

There's another advantage to being slightly less "alone in a room" while writing comedy, and that's the simple fact that a good comedy is significantly easier to sell. Therefore, while comedy might be more difficult to write, writing it well plows the road to success faster that writing dramas or other genres. Why? Remember that this is a business we're talking about, and people want to laugh. Comedies sell tickets year around, and they're welcome in multiplexes throughout the year. If you write big budget action movies, they're probably most welcome in the summer. Moody dramas are fall and winter fare. But comedies keep the popcorn flying out of the bin every day. The industry has a constant appetite for them.

Since a burden shared is a burden halved, a comedic writing partner might aid you in completing not just funnier, more effective scripts, but he or she can also help in piling more scripts. Every story you finish is another arrow in the quiver, another potential sale in the inventory. The writing partner is a chance to double the number of story ideas. And he or she can also provide additional discipline in getting those ideas on the page. If you have to keep a schedule to get writing done, and you're setting meetings especially to do just that, the peer pressure helps to dissolve many of the excuses that might prevent you from working alone in a room.

Overall, I'm not sure I could come up with reasons not to have a good writing partner at your side. Hell, I wish I had one. But maybe I don't play well with others. Fortunately, the comedy writers you're about to meet do. More importantly, I chose them because they are young writers who just broke into the business recently. They're not that far advanced from where you're starting from now. So their experiences are exceptionally relevant. Trust me. What these writers went through, what they did, and what they're doing now — it's all not that far removed from you and your potential future.

Mike Ellis and Pam Falk

Mike Ellis and Pam Falk are an unlikely pair — former lovers who overcame the possible pitfalls of their break-up to become the successful writing team behind the Jennifer Lopez vehicle, *The Wedding Planner*. Before pursuing the career professionally, Ellis wrote in a limited way. He wrote one script in college, and one on his own before he met Falk and started working with her.

"We met at NYU Film School. She couldn't figure out how to sign up for classes. She looked over my shoulder and copied my schedule. We ended up heading out here and began our partnership."

While at NYU, the pair started dating. Falk made a popular film at NYU that got her some attention, while Ellis applied and got into AFI. Ellis still teaches there.

"We were classmates, friends, dating partners — and now writer partners. We dated for about six months — and later drove cross-country. While on that trip, we got an idea for a script. It ended up being the first thing we wrote together that got us our first agent. But, being ex-lovers as writing partners adds an extra, unusual layer. We broke up while we were in rewrites on *Wedding Planner*. We were under contract, and we had to get it done. She moved out of our apartment on Tuesday night, and came back Wednesday morning to do more work on the script. We went through a lot, and people are amazed that we're still writing partners.

"We've tried every possible process, but if only one of us is there, it doesn't work. So we write everything together with me at the keyboard. She's laying around behind me somewhere — pretending she's not writing. We sit down and read the entire thing together aloud — flagging and making notes, et cetera. We do that three or four times for the whole script before we hand it for notes."

How does the pair handle it when the work is simply not flowing well? "On a bad day, when the passion is just not there — it's just not working — it can be really tough. After we sold *Wedding Planner*, we were distracted. The life was sucked out of us with all the stress. We had to plow through and get to the end — go back to the salt mines every day and just get through it. What's great about that process, though, is that it changed the way we worked. It changed our writing process. During those struggles, we were rewriting and rewriting the same pages because we kept reading and re-reading. We don't go back and re-read anymore now until we're done. Get to the end. Until you write the end, you're looking at blank paper. When you finish, then you can rewrite with a feeling of relief that you finished. Even if we have an immediate idea to direct something we just wrote, we make a note and go forward. It helped us stay focused because it took six years for *Wedding Planner* to get to the screen."

The pair goes into note meetings together like a pair of Siamese twins. "Pam and I both feel we need to go through notes together. There are never horrible notes, because even if they can't find a solution, they often correctly find a problem. At least they'd identified an error — even if they might not know how to fix it. It's our job to listen to that and find a solution — to fix it and make it better. What is it about this character, plot point or theme that's calling attention to itself and needing improvement? On our first script sale, when we got notes, it was hard to hear negatives. But that's what I tell my students. The worst thing you can do is sit in a meeting and fight a note. And the fact of the matter is, the executives don't need to work with you. There are plenty of writers out there. Unless you're William Goldman. Then you can do whatever you want."

Now "doing whatever they want" includes assignment writing, but the team is in no hurry. "We're pretty selective in terms of assignments. We don't always like them. Being a second or third writer on something doesn't guarantee you credit or residual checks. It doesn't enthrall us to work on something for six months without credit. We've only taken three assignments in ten years and mostly generate our own material. It's very hard to find assignments that I can be passionate about out there. If you look at the grids on the open writing assignments, you can 200-plus writing assignments, and maybe two that sound appealing. A lot of it is crap."

"We get sent all these script for rewrites. It seems like too much work, but then we realize why it's an open writing assignment. If you're going to do all of that work, you might as well work on your own stuff. Unless the money is really good. But at the end of the day, your integrity is all that counts."

Now Ellis tries to transfer his varied experiences to his students. "What I didn't get at my schools is teachers working in the business. They longed to, or they were retired from the business. We take our practical knowledge and business experience and bring that right into the classroom. We talk about the meetings we have, about the notes sessions. What are the agents telling us? The studio execs? It's important for our students to understand that this has become a business run by the marketing department. No one gives a shit about your story. Nobody cares. They're looking for the lowest common denominator so their boss can get it in three lines. If you can't get it sold like that, you're screwed. Big high-concept ideas that are easy to sell at all levels that people want to make and want to see — they drive the business.

"So intelligence can work against you in screenwriting. If you're smart, you might be better off being a novelist — unless you can separate your intellectual notions from your story and business notions. Bring that kind of practical experience to the table along with some good stories, and you should be fine."

Adam Jay Epstein and Andrew Jacobson

There are those writers who struggle for years to get that first break, working countless unappealing jobs until that magic phone call arrives. Then there's Adam Jay Epstein and Andrew Jacobson. Writers of *Not Another Teen Movie* and an upcoming slate of other motion picture and television comedies, they found success in Hollywood soon after graduating college. Epstein grew up in Long Island, New York and attended Wesleyan University in Connecticut.

"I studied film and economics," Esptein said. "After college, I moved out here to Los Angeles knowing no one the summer after college. I really didn't know what I wanted to do in the business because the closest I ever came to Hollywood was the Universal Studios tour." He began temping and wrote during his evenings. On one of his temp gigs, he met Jacobson, and the two became friends.

Jacobson grew up in Wisconsin and attended the University of Wisconsin in Madison. He studied journalism and wanted to try Hollywood after college. "I thought that I wanted to be a writer. Like Adam, I was working as an assistant and wrote a couple scripts after work."

Epstein was staying at UCLA for temporary summer housing. When he saw "an opportunity to latch onto a smart and successful guy in Jacobsen," they started writing together. "We'd work together in the office until 6. We'd take twenty minutes for dinner, then head off to a coffee shop to write all night."

Jacobsen added, "We tried a shoddy, short, spoof film to try to get some attention around town for our scripts, and that additionally led to us getting management and the writing assignment on *Not Another Teen Movie*."

"We did it backwards. We started our career with rewrites and are only now selling original material. But I think it is possible to have a different level of passion for your own material as opposed to a rewrite, so we're always working on original scripts."

Off their recent feature success, the team wants to transition to television. They're working on an update of the 1970s classic, *Three's Company*. In their sitcom pilot, a young guy moves in with two ex-girlfriends, and hilarity ensues.

"We liked action movies," Epstein said. "But we shifted into comedy because we're young guys who everyone sees as 'young funny guys.' We found out that comedy was scary — the toughest genre to write. As a writer and someone who loves movies, I think I always want to be doing something different and writing in every genre. But as a team, I think we do well at comedy set pieces. We tried different genres, but none of them was sticking. Finally, we tried comedy. That drew the attention of our managers."

Their work on *Not Another Teen Movie* provided a fast turn-around. The team got the job in August of 2000, wrote their script in September, and the film was green-lit in November. Shooting started by late January 2001.

"So many people have five or six unproduced scripts, but our first went," Jacobsen added. "So we wished we'd had a few more unproduced to sell. But our work is coming together now. But we feel like we haven't yet made it. Though we've done a little bit of everything in the business, we still feel like we're on the fringes."

"We're constantly in a process of coming up with new ideas. But we're pretty busy on assignments. We hope the TV series will go, and we'll shoot the pilot in January."

Peter Speakman and Michael M. B. Galvin

In many ways, Peter Speakman and Michael M. B. Galvin are the "Odd Couple" of screenwriters. Before coming together as a writing team and putting together the spec sale script, *Scrabble*, Speakman graduated from UCLA and was working ten years for the president of Dimension Films. Galvin was from New York and kicked around after graduating from college — playing in punk rock bands. So you had the west coast straight-laced corporate entertainment employee teaming up with the east coast starving musician to write comedies, while their very partnership sounds like the premise of a Hollywood laugher.

"I felt kind of blind working alone — always giving people stuff to read and looking for guidance," Galvin said.

Speakman added, "When I was writing alone, I'd never give anyone anything to read because I didn't want the input. So both ways are difficult to work out because you're getting too much or too little input from the outside."

Before their partnership, Michael wrote an unpublished novel entitled "Talk about Sex." The pair adapted the book into a comedy that sold and is now available on video as the film *Blowing Smoke*. Off that action, they were approached by a commercial director that got the pair into *Scrabble*, a comedy romance set in the world of competitive board games.

"They bought the script, and a year and a half later they asked us to rewrite it," Michael said. "And they continue to ask us to rewrite it. It never seems to end, and it can be tough to maintain enthusiasm over something like that over five years. Different people come into the project, and have their input. They're not as invested in the project as we've been, and we feel like we're the most involved. It's hard not to be frustrated as writers because you want more control, naturally. But I would still encourage people to get into this business. We have a great time writing. You do get strange demands from people, but that can be part of the fun.

"People buy scripts every day — from first time writers every day. And that should be encouraging. It doesn't have to be a big thing, but it's happening every day — so it can happen to you."

During the actual writing process, Michael said they're both in the room while typing. "We take a stab at it back and forth, taking turns. I personally think it's a great way to do comedy because it's hard to see if something is funny unless someone else is there to react to it."

"We know of other people who do it other ways," Peter added. "We tried to write at the same time on different computers in the same room, but we end up getting wrapped up in one version or the other."

"I don't get how people write without partners," Michael said. "Writers in general want to please readers, but there are times when one of us wants to strangle them, and the other is there to stop him."

While the pair found success with comedy, they have ambitions to branch out.

"We wrote other stuff. We wrote a western. We're both fans of crime fiction. But most of what we do becomes dark comedy. And we talk about directing, but I think we're people of the page — and directing is a daunting task."

I would add that directing is no more daunting than starting a career as a comedy writing tandem, but that's a topic for a different book. For now, we'll move on and keep adding people to our writing room and examine the experiences of professionals writing for television dramas, situation comedies, and reality television. While looking at this area of the Hollywood writing business might make this book's title slightly less relevant for a while, all of those disciplines offer an amount of opportunities to aspiring writers that the movie business can't always match.

section three

The Writing Staff

In the early morning hours before the main event, there
occurred the fulfillment of a life-long dream:
To write with the bulls.

chapter eight

In From the Bullpen:
Pressure in the TV Sitcom's Writer Room

It's ironic. I prefer to write my screenplays, books, and magazine articles alone. It's always been that way, and I imagine it always will be that way. The creative conversations, motivations, and organizations that arise in my head during the writing process would be far too difficult to explain or outline to anyone else, so I bang away at the keys on my own. However, and this is the ironic bit, the most pleasant writing memory of my career was a short gig I enjoyed for a funny little show that never really took off in the form intended. I don't know if I'll ever be lucky enough to recreate that experience anywhere else in the industry, so it's precious to me.

I got a job as a writer's assistant on the Black Entertainment Television show, *Comicview*. You might know the show as it is now — simply a down-and-dirty urban stand-up comedy show. However, at the time, the network wanted to expand the show and maybe create a spin-off that would feature sketches and a regular cast of multi-racial comic actors (a la *Saturday Night Live*, *In Living Color*, or *Mad TV*). Since the show was primarily for an African American audience, the writing staff and the cast reflected that sensibility. However, there was a need to diversify the staff. Fortunately, the outstanding, upbeat, and supportive producers of the show at that time (comedy writers Jesse Collins and Greg Fields) allowed me to step up and write for the show.

Unfortunately, changes at the executive level at the cable network changed the direction of the show before it even aired. To the best of my knowledge, our sketches never aired. All of those long hours in the writer's room and all of the hard work by the cast and crew (not to mention the money invested in the production) more or less went to waste. Sure, the paychecks cleared, but it was a painful disappointment to see the show treated with such little respect. Was it funny? Yes. However, it wasn't the baby of the new executives entering the picture, and that situation often means death for the projects of the old regime.

What do you do in such a situation? You try to take pride in your work and your effort. You treasure the fun you had doing the work and try to stay in touch with the friends you made on the staff. Most importantly, you fight not to grow bitter. There are far too many people adopting that attitude in the business, and it can't do you any good as it saps your energy and makes you less appealing as a would-be employee. Finally, you get right back on the horse and look for your next job immediately. You don't want to dwell on frustrations.

First things first.
That said, how do you get that first job writing for TV comedy? One of the "easiest" and most popular routes is seeking work as a writer's assistant. An assistant gets to play a small part in the creative process while watching over a veteran writer's shoulder as big-time Hollywood marches past. What exactly does a writer's assistant do? It depends on the writer or writers employing the assistant. On sitcoms, writing assistants sit in on meetings and take note of revisions during brainstorming sessions or script reviews by the show's producers. For assistants helping out one-hour drama or feature writers, duties can range from interesting creative tasks and involvement to

clerical tasks to personal business. It's all based on how the writer handles his or her work and life.

The most interesting and challenging duties a writer's assistant can hope for are revisions and research. The latter is obvious. If a screen-writer is making six or seven figures per script, writing time is money — a lot of money. It's much easier for that writer to pay someone else to examine historical texts, list types of modern weapons or discover if this week's script title has ever been used before. As far as revisions go, don't think "creative." Think "saving the writer work." When the A-list writer performs a script revision, he or she is pulling down a hefty check to rewrite a screenplay. As a writing assistant, when you perform revisions for that writer, you're catching typos, misspellings, or continuity errors.

In some cases with older writers, revision means conquering the veteran writer's technophobia. Some current screenwriters on the tail end of their careers came into the business composing their work on typewriters. Some even wrote their first drafts by hand and let some-one from the studio typing pool or a "Kelly Girl" bang it into script format. Writer's assistants are this era's answer to the typing pool. They may write their scripts in some old-fashioned form and ask you to type them into the computer. When older writers look at a Mac or PC screen and see word processing software like MS Word or WordPerfect (or even specific screenwriting programs like Final Draft or Movie Magic), they may need you to make sense of it for them. Do it — quickly! You'll spare the wizened scribe a mild emotional attack, and you'll save yourself the story of how, in the old days, you didn't need these new-fangled computers to write a picture... and how the writer used to walk to the studio in the snow every day, uphill, both ways, et cetera.

Some of a writer's assistant duties can stretch into the clerical realm. You could be asked to sit in on meetings to take notes from studio execs. Or, if they tape the meeting, you might have to transcribe the notes. That allows the screenwriter to think on his or her feet — and to look important in front of the studio execs. They all have assistants, and if a writer wants to be a player, he or she has to have one, too. Whether or not you want one when you make your break is entirely up to you.

If a writer is working on a single spec or writing on assignment, a writer's assistant's life can prove fairly smooth. However, more often than not, a writer is working on multiple projects. Any one of a number of stories in various stages of development could be submitted all around town. Or a sitcom writer might be working on multiple scripts for an extended season. One script might be approaching final draft form, while another is at the treatment or breakdown stage. It's often the assistant's job to track all those drafts to make sure the right title and correct draft goes to the right producer.

In some rare, dreaded cases, a writer's assistant's duties slide into the sordid realm of personal assistant duties. The jobs are separate, and in a perfect world, they stay that way. Still, on occasion, even the most skilled writer's assistant will be asked to make a delivery, order lunch, or pick up a Prozac prescription. Those duties can be a blow to an educated assistant's fragile ego, but you need to perform them anyway. Personally, I was fortunate because the producer on our sketch comedy show would show me a little respect and human consideration — just with little things. For example, if he sent me out to Starbucks for him or anyone else on staff, he'd slip me a couple extra bucks so I could grab something, too. Even if you get less than glamorous jobs or a less than polite boss, tough it out and consider them favors for someone helping you to pay your bills. If you're taking care of far more personal business than creative, then you may wish to look for a new gig.

So, a writer's assistant position is a true "pay your dues" sort of gig. But what's in it for you — besides a paycheck ranging from $10 to $15 per hour? Hopefully, you can pick up some vital first-hand education on how the industry really works. An assistantship allows the young writer to watch the slings and arrows of writing for Hollywood from the battle's sidelines without having to wield a weapon before he or she is ready It's sort of like playing squire to the established writer's knight. You can pick up insight on the draft and revision process, the pitch routine, writing on assignment, and the screenwriting market-place. You can also prepare yourself for some of the less pleasant aspects of professional screenwriting, such as dealing with impatient, inconsistent producers and the endless mill of studio notes.

If your boss likes you (which is never a given if you consider how temperamental writers can be), he or she might be willing to read your work and refer it to producers, show runners, and agents looking for new talent. But don't fool yourself. No writer will take bread off his or her table so they can give your career a break. You will get the crumbs the established writer doesn't want, but those are crumbs you probably can't eat now without such an opportunity.

Finally, if you end up working for a writer you admire, you may find inspiration or technique in his or her craft that improves your own screenplays. No writer's assistant holds such a job for the sheer joy of assisting! You take the support role in hope that it will lead to your own writing opportunities down the road. If you're lucky enough to fall in with a writer willing to serve as a mentor on the side, the job might just make you a better writer.

Breaking into the country club...

Once you've done your time as a writer's assistant, you hope to earn your first shot writing an episode. Beginning writers can earn about $3000 a week for a 26-week contract. If the show runner chooses to assign additional scripts, you can earn an additional $11,000 to about $18,000, depending on the show. Of course, you get residuals, but the amount all depends on the next WGA strike.

Of course, you need to get there first. And in addition to the writing assistant route, you must write a spec script. Actually, you're going to need more than one because no one can write one script and think he or she is a professional. An outstanding spec will serve as your calling card to the industry and should open doors for you. But it must be excellent — on a par with the top professional work. No, you'll never get paid for it. No one will buy it because you never write a spec for the show you want to write for — merely the genre of show you want to write. You can never assume that you can write a show better than those who created it or currently write it for TV. Fortunately, you're starting out and have no chance of writing for the top sitcoms on the air currently. So you're free to write for your favorite, big-time show as a sample to newer shows that might want to staff up with younger talent.

Obviously, whatever spec you choose to write should be very popular (hence known to any potential reader) and a program that you like. Write what makes you laugh because your enthusiasm and inspired humor has a better chance of coming through on the page. Plus, you must write what you know and you should know your favorite shows absolutely cold. But avoid writing a spec that's one of the all-time stand-bys — any show that's been on for more than three seasons —

because would-be readers like agents and producers read countless examples from those shows.

While writing your spec, make sure not to introduce new characters. Work with only what works for the show you're writing as it's created. Write with only what's already there. And never try to "push the envelope" by leading the show's characters in some new and strange direction. You might think you're being creative, but you're actually demonstrating that you don't really know the show. That's a killer. Finally, make absolutely sure that you're not repeating a story the show already aired. Again, you're writing in the box, but looking for something in that box that hasn't been done.

Obviously, your spec script must be formatted correctly. More importantly, it must look exactly like scripts from the show's production office. Since many shows have little quirks and tricks on the page to identify their scripts, it's best if you got actual production copies from script stores in Hollywood. Or, if you're out of town, you can get them online. It's all about getting past the show's gatekeepers and giving them no reason to say no before they've even read your script.

Down and Dirty

What do you do with your script once you wrote it? Who should review it? Who should read it? That's an entirely different book. Indeed, entire texts exist that deal exclusively with breaking into the sitcom game. I just wanted to get you started and point you in the right direction. However, I would point out some painful truths about the game before you step into it — because that's precisely what I intended this book to do.

Always keep in mind that it's very competitive in Hollywood, and only significant tenacity will get you into the door. However, no amount of toughness and determination will help you if you don't live in L.A. and are already in your mid-30s before you begin looking to write in comedy. You must live in LA to write for comedic television because it is an office job on location or on the lot, and you must be younger than most professional writers working successfully.

Ah, yes... the "y" word — "younger." Amidst all the areas of television, sitcom writing slants most to youth for the simple fact that producers want writers in tune with a younger demographic (the traditional audience for the hippest and newest sitcoms). Also, they're looking for insanely dedicated artists who will more or less enslave themselves to the show. Because of last-minute rewrites, long work days extended by endless note sessions, and rehearsals going on into the wee hours, producers don't want writers with families. They want men and women who can sleep in their offices after a long day and hit it first thing the next morning after a bagel and three coffees.

So, with the emphasis on age being so dominant, it was only a matter of time before the older writers falling out of favor unpacked their lawsuits. Unfortunately, those lawsuits failed. In 2003, a California Superior Court judge dismissed a class-action lawsuit brought by more than 175 writers alleging that television networks, Hollywood studios, and talent agencies discriminate against writers over forty. Judge Charles W. McCoy, Jr. ruled that some of the alleged violations occurred outside the statute of limitations and that the writers first must prove their claims on an individual basis before they can show an industry-wide pattern of discrimination. The ruling left open the possibility that the writers could re-file their claims individually. In short, the judge stated that there was not yet a clear enough proven pattern of discriminatory behavior to allow a class action suit. However, any single writer who considers himself or herself a victim of age discrimination in violation of federal law — and who holds clear evidence of such behavior — can file his or her case.

Some twenty-eight writers filed their original suit in October 2000. The action claimed more than $200 million in damages because Hollywood studios and agencies had allegedly relegated older scribes to a professional limbo (or "gray list") because of their age. In other professions (except for professional athletes and a few other careers that require a great amount of physical strength, speed, endurance, or agility), advancing age is often an advantage, while youth is eyed with concern until it is trained and seasoned. You would rather leave your life in the hands of an experienced neurosurgeon instead of the young intern. You would prefer that your house be built by a journeyman carpenter instead of his or her apprentice.

Unfortunately, these days Hollywood (especially the television industry) looks at age as a detriment for a writer and looks for progressively younger and younger talent to staff productions. Although the progression of years and trials would seem to insure greater skill and instincts for a writer, Hollywood fears those same years distance them from younger viewers tuning in for the hottest programs. Perhaps Mark Twain wrote his best work later in his life. Certainly, Shakespeare's tenth play was better than his first. But neither of them could work for *Friends* or *Malcolm in the Middle* in this era because they're not in their twenties and fresh out of college.

Hollywood's ageism began in earnest during the 1980s. Before that time, successful film and TV writers were working well into their sixties, maintaining careers similar in length to other professions.

Nevertheless, the '80s introduced a heavy emphasis on demographics and audience marketing statistics into entertainment programming and development. It became a common belief among executives and producers eager to capture the advertising dollar of the all-powerful 18-32 demographic that writers had to fall within range to write for that age set.

If you can get yourself to L.A. and still fall within the acceptable age range, the door to Hollywood comedy could be open to you. To help show you the way, I offer Dave Collard — a writer who fought his way into the writer's bullpen and helped write one of the most popular primetime animated sitcoms of the last few years, *Family Guy*.

Dave Collard

It might seem unusual for a supposedly straight-laced, Madison Avenue type to have a sense of humor. It seems even stranger for a former economics major with TV comedy writing experience to write a compelling crime thriller. But Dave Collard seems to enjoy taking the less-traveled route.

"After college, I figured I'd set out to try my luck at Wall Street," Collard said. "But I happened upon some screenwriting courses and got my first decent grades in those classes. I decided to come out here after college — not knowing fortunately how many other people had that same idea."

While writing his first specs, Collard got a job on Seth McFarland's animated series, *Family Guy*, as a writing assistant. He worked his way onto staff and wrote episodes of that popular Fox Show — earning the attention of an agent. His career took off from there.

The one thing that makes an animated half-hour show different from a typical three-camera sitcom is the length of the entire production process — about nine months. Standard live-action shows can go from script to shoot in less than a month. For a show like *Family Guy*, a season would start in June and July with the writing staff meeting and talking about their ideas. They discuss general areas to cover, and those concepts go up on a bulletin board. Then writers start focusing on which areas sound more promising.

The entire staff would break down a story and list several needs per act. Then the head writer would assign the story to a writer or writing team. So the group develops the plotline, but individual writers or staff teams would have to focus in and be ready to break out the story. They would be sent off to do an outline, and then could include certain jokes they envisioned during the development process. As it moved along, the executive producer and show runner would work through it.

According to Collard, "The writer works on the first draft for about two weeks. Then the first draft is reviewed by the entire writer's room, the head writer, and the executive producer before the original script takes it back for revision. Then, if everybody thinks the script is pretty good, the script would go into the writer's room for an overhaul with the whole staff. The writer's assistant puts it up on computer screens for everyone to review, and the entire group refines it — especially with the jokes that need polishing. Everyone has the same goal of shining up the show and making it as funny as it can be.

"That's the process of an animated show. Then the script would go to audio recording with the actors. The producer, director, and animators would then create the show. It'd go away for six months, come back for polish, then go away again for final editing and production.

"The tough part is keeping that story in your head for all of that time. You'd work on other projects during that six months, so you'd get a little distance on it. Then you'd have to come back to it months later and get yourself back in that space. But you're always working on something else while you're working that nine-month process. You do a rewrite, another episode, et cetera."

As for sitcoms, the development, writing, and production process takes three to four weeks — and that includes last minute rewrites. Animated sitcoms have just as many tough deadlines as a traditional show, but writers are working on multiple projects, spread out over time.

Collard added, "*Family Guy* had a great atmosphere in the writer's room while I was on the show. Day to day, it was a great place to work. I was working with ten or twelve men and women that I really liked. Everyone was really talented. We all got along really well. Most days, it was great because you're trying to crack each other up — just lounging and trying to come up with jokes. It's a lot like when you're in college, sitting up all night bullshitting with your friends. Except I was getting paid."

"But you had to stay sharp because you wanted to make sure that you got a couple funny jokes into the script. If you were slacking that day or not locked in, you'd know it because nothing of yours would end up on the page. You'd have to come back the next day and lock in to get more of your material in there. That made for some good competitiveness to get jokes on the screen — to make the show stronger."

Collard just finished a feature for Disney. "I like the hours of working on your own on a feature, but I miss the camaraderie of being in the room and working with the guys from *Family Guy*. I guess that I'd love to stay on writing features — and figure out a way to work on a show with the guys from *Family Guy* again."

I wanted to include Collard because he had to make the transition from the writing team environment to the "alone in a room" phase. How was it going from the constant support, interaction, and feedback of multiple comedy writers to the more isolated, yet controlled environment of writing on one's own?

When it came time to write features, Collard was always working on his own scripts while working on *Family Guy*. "Once we got our agents, I showed them this spec I'd been working on. They took it out in October 2000, and MGM picked it up. From there, I continued to work on *Family Guy*, and kept up new drafts of that spec at the studios."

In July 2001, director Carl Franklin came on board, and Collard's script evolved into *Out of Time*. Once Denzel Washington was attached, the project was green-lit. "I was lucky with that project because MGM let me rewrite it with their notes. They didn't fire me to bring on another writer. And Carl was very good to work with because he knew what he wanted. In the end, it was three years from the day when it opened from when it was bought. So that's a three-year break into the industry for me.

"I'd say breaking into Hollywood is like picking up a combination lock and randomly twisting it back and forth until it opens. So many things can go wrong before your project find its way to the screen."

While Collard wrote for years as part of the *Family Guy* writing team, he enjoys writing his screenplays on his own. "I was writing film alone and writing with *Family Guy* on staff in the writer's room. After doing that all day, it was nice to go home and do it my way without checking with anyone to see if it's okay."

"I try to keep banker's hours. I work out of an office because I need to get out of the house — separating church and state. I go nine to five, and I unplug the Internet. During those eight hours, I might be doing research, development, notes or phone calls. But I keep a stream of consciousness MS Word document going all the time. I ask myself rhetorical questions and try to think it through while I work. That way, during a first draft, I try to get seven pages a day. As a boss, I'm not the hardest guy on me. So I keep that amount flexible."

Collard added that if he'd known how tough breaking into Hollywood was, he might not have attempted it. "I never had outlets to inform me of the competition — ignorance was bliss. But it's settled down a little now because the $4 million spec sales are gone."

As for you other writers who are aware of the challenges awaiting you in Hollywood, Collard advises you to give yourselves a reasonable amount of time to find their way. "Whether you're writing TV or film, consider your first scripts graduate school. Give yourself a couple of years to learn your craft. You need to be realistic that it's going to take time. And you need to be out here in L.A. You can write from somewhere else, but you need to be here to learn the business. Write from anywhere to discover your voice, but you need to be able to meet people and be accessible until you reach a level of success that allows you to live anywhere. So when you're serious, come out here and give yourself time — because there's no such thing as the true overnight success."

The Writer takes a staff job.

chapter nine

Staff Infection:
The Rigors of Writing TV Drama

The world of one-hour television dramas is almost as diverse as the feature market because there is such a variety of shows on the air. It's more than a question of genre with cop shows airing alongside family dramas and sci-fi adventures. Different markets are involved, including network, cable, and syndicated shows. All of these shows are made under wildly different budgets and varying conditions. One show might be shot at great expense on a Hollywood studio lot, while others are shot in Australia, New Zealand, or South Africa on a shoestring budget. Finally, some of these shows (especially syndicated hours) are more open to younger, less accomplished writers as they need to fill staff jobs with less than top dollar talent.

As for the inside process of how a show works, it's practically identical to the sitcom operating procedure. Shows go from pitch to pilot to production and (hopefully) to pick-up. Writers break into the business through the same process of serving as writing assistants or PAs while writing their spec scripts. The only differences might be in how many episodes a writer would tackle a season, since a one-hour TV episode is like writing half of a feature — instead of a seventeen-minute sitcom episode. Also, the drama world includes syndicated and cable shows that may hire writers on assignment — leaving you to work at home while you simply send your scripts to some far-away office.

M. A. Lovretta

To introduce you to the world of TV dramas, I chose younger writers who are just breaking into that world. They write for different kinds of shows under special conditions, but their experiences are vital to any up-and-coming scribe that looks to write for dramatic television. We begin with M. A. Lovretta, a Canadian writer who wrote for *Relic Hunter* and *Mutant X*. I know that some of what you've read thus far was drenched in doom and gloom, but I don't want you to get discouraged. To that end, I have the ultimate remedy — a good old-fashioned, up-and-coming success story. Lovretta enjoys the kind of rapid-fire success that can make immature and less-accomplished writers rotten with envy. But before you delve too deeply into that deadly sin, take my word for it: She's far too nice a woman to warrant any such disdain.

A native of Canada residing somewhere "aboot" Toronto, Lovretta currently walks the less-traveled television road of syndicated, one-hour drama. While most aspiring TV scribblers dream of the big network bucks on *Friends* or *Law and Order*, someone has to write the weekend afternoon and late-night sci-fi and action adventure shows out there. Whether it's Arthur Conan Doyle's *The Lost World*, *She Spies*, or *Poltergeist — The Legacy*, the syndicated market is an area often overlooked by young writers. Such shows are less prevalent now than in recent years as budgetary belts tighten across the industry, but these shows are still out there.

How did Lovretta go from Winslow College across the river from Detroit to her consistent and building writing success? Optioning a screenplay in college helped.

"I was too ambitious and impatient in college," Lovretta said. "I knew what I wanted to do, and classes in geology weren't going to get me there. I went to my adviser in the film and TV department and told him that I was thinking of leaving the program. He agreed that in film and television academic programs, the work and experience is key. The degree is less important. He suggested that I stay and adapt the thirty-minute script I wrote as part of the program into a feature."

Lovretta evolved that story into *The Fishing Trip*. After she finished the script and wrapped her time at Windsor, her professor handed her a letter. She thought it might be a glowing recommendation letter for her future pursuits, but it turned out to be an option offer on her first feature. She was off and running before graduation. The option rolled over into a purchase and full production. The film, which deals with two sisters struggling to come to terms with an abusive father, soon found its way onto the short list of major festivals. Amidst all of this, she made calls to production companies looking for a job — even occasionally offering to donate time just to gain experience.

One of her college professors ended up optioning *The Fishing Trip*, and the completed film eventually entered the Canadian equivalent of AFI. Meanwhile, she kept writing in Canada. She wrote a TV script there that got sold and went into production in Canada. But, according to Lovretta, writers can't live off features in Canada. But the doors her previous work opened led to a conversation with a network executive connected with someone developing a TV series called *Relic Hunter*. The first series gig led to a staff job on *The Associates* (a Canadian show) and, eventually, *Mutant X*.

"I have very commercial tastes as a writer, and my tastes tend to seem more American that Canadian," Lovretta explained. "My natural sensibilities are standard entertainment. I've never felt like I was selling out writing adventure or science fiction. I have friends who go that route and agonize about it. I like popcorn movies. I think that it's something that divides writers fairly early. Some of us have novel sensibilities, and some of us have comic book sensibilities. I had more of the taste of a fifteen-year-old boy. But, with writing, it's possible to stretch yourself beyond your personal preferences. I haven't really had to do that yet. One constant for my work is that I'm drawn to a strong female protagonist."

Lovretta sees her career path running from television to features to novels. "As a consumer, I don't pick between them or consider one superior to another. I watch film and TV, and it amazes me that people admit which they prefer in meetings. Why would you say something like, "I don't like TV. I don't like movies..." while they're trying to get a job. Fortunately, in Canada, once your foot is in the door, it's easier to make a living. In Hollywood, during your first meetings, they ask what you do before you've even done it. They want to pigeonhole you as soon as possible. You open your own options, while closing others. In Canada, it's not the case. The business is more fluid, maybe because there are less writers to choose from here. You can jump from one-hour to sitcom to MOW to feature. In the end, your career is a commodity. It's how you market yourself. But your creative output is your own perspective. Making a buck is a good thing, but you have to satisfy yourself creatively too."

To satisfy herself, Lovretta sees herself writing features soon because "while they can be a bigger risk at the studio level, they provide a much bigger canvas. If you watch enough movies and TV shows, you can get into that rhythm of writing either form. I always keep in my head for features — staying very directed and maintaining my own internal sense of timing. I hold onto ideas that are good and commercial because I'm not willing to risk revealing or losing them. Fortunately, I've been working so steadily that I haven't had a moment to make it a priority."

"I'll save novels for when the industry decides I'm too old to write for it."

On the TV side, Lovretta views her next step as a series creator — hopefully for American TV. "I'd love to be the person who created the show and was caretaking it. But it would have to be an American show because nothing on Canadian TV will have a budget. The more you get into the business, the more power you want. Whether it's business or creative, I can be a control freak. Right now, I'm happy working for other people."

It might seem that Lovretta hasn't struggled — that she was making money writing before she got out of college and kept the momentum up until now. Does she think that's an advantage or a disadvantage? Is there internal pressure to keep up that momentum, or can she play around a bit because she's professionally or financially secure?

"Well, first define 'struggle.' Do you mean the typical romantic notion of a struggling writer, throwing blood, sweat, and adjectives onto the page while living in bohemian poverty hoping against hope that money, fame, or at least another job will come out of it? Why would you presume I escaped that particular little hell? An indie option fee in Canada is usually about enough to treat yourself to McDonalds."

"Looked at in another way, in the year and a half that I worked on the script for what became my first movie (without anything remotely resembling real pay in the interim), hundreds of other young 'wannabe' writers were doing the same — writing their first screenplay. They were sweating over every word as it appeared on the page, second-guessing their abilities or right to even attempt such a lofty goal. They were worrying that at the end, once the last key was stroked and page printed, nothing would come from their screenplay. Or worse, people would read it, loathe it, and the sham of their talents would be proven on a more public scale. That's exactly what was happening to me over that same span. The only difference is that they were toiling on spec scripts and mine had been optioned. Just because you have a director or producer involved, and just because you're fairly assured that your opus is going to be shot does not make it any less stressful. Nor does it demand any less effort from you. In fact, I'd argue the imposing of real-world deadlines and expectations requires more effort from novice writers unused to such pressures. They would rather just retreat to the coffee shop and talk about how they're writing a movie than put in the all-nighters actually required."

"It also doesn't guarantee you success, legitimacy, or even a clear hint as to what your next career move should be at the end of it. Subtract any illusion of monetary recompense, and yes, I had fairly early success. The film was made, premiered at the Toronto International Film Fest and followed at a few others internationally, got a small distributor, and even got nominated for two Genies — the Canadian Oscars (though not for the screenplay, but for best original song). But then, nothing. I didn't even have an agent by the end of it. And there was no hint as to how, after investing nearly two years of my life, I could go about making a living, finally, from my talents. I wasn't really much farther ahead. So, yes. I struggled. I would argue it's impossible to write without struggling — usually with internal/psychological/creative issues."

Does being comfortable financially make her work easier? "Vastly. I'm thrilled and grateful to have had a string of good jobs lately, and always work hard to ensure the next one, because a lump of money in the bank empowers you to turn down potentially deadening, offensive, or stressful gigs that you would otherwise have to take. In short, there's nothing like knowing your rent is covered to free you to make the right — or at least thoughtful and empowered — career moves."

While you and I might face writing dry spells, does Lovretta go through similar experiences while completing all of her work?

"Whoa, Nelly, do I. Now, I assume you mean creative and not employment dry patches because they're unrelated. The creative sort is more disturbing to me. It happened to me once and I still have the shivers when I think of it. Basically: my first two years as a TV writer I had a pretty busy spell. I'd written about twelve to fourteen scripts of varying length, most of them produced or otherwise paid for and some of them spec samples. At the end of those two great years, when the Canadian series I was also staffing at the time ended, I was wiped out. And, I must add, feeling like a weakling to be tired out under that minimal load having heard often enough about the freakish outputs of the David E. Kelley and Aaron Sorkin types.

"I decided not to do any work or hurry to take any freelance gigs immediately knowing my bank account was stocked and my creativity was at a definite low. Soon two months became four, and I realized that I wasn't avoiding writing because of a hedonist decision to relax but because I had nothing to write. For the first time in my life, there was silence in my head. No voices, and no little pithy threads of dialogue I could choose to follow and see where they led. It was like, for lack of a better image, being mentally deaf. I sunk into a depression and terror unlike any I hope to experience again. All I can say right now is that my brain was balled up like a fist, and it took time for it to unclench enough to be creative and productive again. I think much of it was caused by the fact that, of those twelve to fourteen scripts, only one was an original world of my making. The others were me following or fitting into someone else's creative vision. That's stifling and potentially damaging. I will never take inspiration for granted again. I still don't understand exactly where it comes from, but I can't stand the thought of ever being without it again."

With all of that stress piling up so early, was Lovretta ever able to appreciate the success she had early? Or did she think that's just the way it was supposed to be?

"I'm not successful. That's how I think I'll always look at it even when that becomes a ridiculously blind thing to say. I don't mean that as an insult to anyone starting out and still struggling to get to where I am. It's more just a philosophical worldview thing. There's always another, more accomplished level I aspire to, more things to learn, mentors to meet. As a consequence, I have literally had an inability to focus on or appreciate the successes I've had so far.

"That said, it would have been exponentially harder for me to achieve the things I've achieved if I'd known how ridiculously, statistically improbable they were and chosen to shoot for them anyway. In fact, I made more leaps and bounds in my career at the beginning than lately because I didn't know what the hell I was doing or was up against there. I didn't realize it was slightly cocky to even dare it. An example:

When I was about twenty-four, with nothing but an indie film behind me that few TV people had heard of, I decided to make the leap to television. When I had my very first courtesy meeting with a wonderful TV executive in Canada who had yet to read my work, he asked me an innocent question. 'Do you have any ideas of your own?' (Meaning: Are you planning to be a staff writer permanently, or do you hope to be a creator one day?) But what I *thought* he meant was, 'You look about twelve — are you a complete airhead? Or, is there something more than perfume under that Big Hair?'

"So, of course, I reacted by blurting out the only two series ideas I'd ever had and ended up leaving that room with a series development deal before I'd ever even written a single TV script. Would that have happened to me otherwise? No. I know myself: I would have kept those ideas secret because I was afraid of pitching. For every success I've accidentally had, I've sabotaged myself twice as often. Not finishing spec scripts for my agents, not telling them a fabulous movie idea I have because I'm afraid they'll want me to pitch it in the U.S. and, then, what if I fail? I've even had a second feature script finished as of six years ago that I've never shown my reps because it doesn't feel right yet. I'm not by any means original in this. Most writers I know are their own worst enemies when it comes to crafting a career, either through a lack of social skills or a surplus or deficiency of aggressiveness or ego. If anyone figures out a cure for this, I'd love to hear it."

I digress here just for a moment to suggest that I am crafting just such a cure on these very educational pages. But I don't want to seem arrogant, so I'll turn the focus back to Lovretta. How does she keep the pressure on herself to keep evolving and improving when the status quo is obviously working for her?

"I'm all about the self-pressure. There's usually a pattern to any good career turn I've encountered such as selling a movie. It includes:

1. A few hours of drug-like elation and pride. 'Woo-hoo! I rock! Who da writer?'
2. A few days of panic. 'Did I make any wrong or stupid moves? Is this deal going to bite me in the ass?
3. Weeks of depression. Shit, this thing is actually getting made now. I have so much work to do to get this to a place I'm happy with now. For some reason, I'm suddenly so unbelievably *tired*.
4. An eternity of general discomfort. 'It's been years since I wrote script X. I knew nothing back then. There're so many things I wish I'd known how to do better.'

It's something my mother has noted... When something cool happens like an award nomination, it's usually like pulling teeth to get me to volunteer the information to anyone. I think in some twisted way I'm afraid any self-acknowledgment of success will 'dull' me somehow, deplete some sort of underdog-hunger instinct or desire to push myself to rise above the rest. If I think I'm a failure, I'll be more determined to make myself a success. Or so the twisted internal logic goes. Besides, overconfidence just makes you an obnoxious ass at parties, because every room has got a minimum ten people that are doing way better than you."

Since she's worked both ways, does Lovretta prefer working in her home office or in a production office setting? "The idea of having to write 'in the room' was a shocking and rude awakening for me. Personally, I hate writing outside of my home office, and I find the work I produce outside of it is never as good because part of my mind is never fully relaxed and immersed. It's too hard for me to concentrate at the office. In the best work situation I've had thus far, my boss knew my routine and we came to an understanding. I'd always be in the office for all meetings, but when my script was next on the block, I'd write at home any afternoon I could be spared. That worked best for me. Otherwise, I'm in the office all day meeting and kicking ideas around with the team. Then, I go home and write, often non-stop, until the morning when it's time to do it all over again. Needless to say, I tend to get sick by the end of staffing season."

When it's not going well, how does she bear down to get the work done, regardless of whether we're talking her own MOW or an episode on a hard deadline?

"Three words: Fear of disappointing — which is basically fear of failure, but with a more personal face on it. It drives me through most blocks and explains why I am five times more productive/expedient on scripts I'm hired to write over scripts I'm doing on spec. I am a writer before all other things. Personal commitments get thrown aside without hesitation to ensure I meet a deadline. I don't say this with any pride. I wish I knew another way to do it. As for mental tricks, when I'm hitting a wall and coming up empty, I have a little sign above my computer that says, "It doesn't have to be perfect — yet." I find this freeing, because it alleviates my perfectionism (the source of most of my mental blocks) without ignoring it. The key is remembering the process. Things aren't meant to be great the first draft, or the Guild's pay scale wouldn't take us through two more steps."

I seem to remember me saying something similar along those lines during the revision chapter. You never want to be crippled by expectations of perfection or fear of revision. The only area in which my style and procedure might deviate from Lovretta's is in the drama department. I can manage to come up for air during on-assignment writing because I pride myself on always remaining calm. Why? Because, like Lovretta, I went through a period of severe blocks and feared I'd have to change careers. I panicked. So, once I overcame that panic, I resolved never to descend into it again. I don't engage in the "drama" school of writing on deadline in which you forgo bathing, eating, friends, family, and sleep to get the work done. I attempt to stay balanced. I don't think it's better or worse than Lovretta's style. It's just different approaches for different writers.

Jay Beattie and Dan Dworkin

Story editors on ABC's *Dragnet*, this pair started out on the show's premiere season as staff writers. Dworkin provided the outstanding funeral script sale story earlier. Now he and his partner show how their first full year writing in Hollywood is a textbook examination of how impossibly wild the business can be for those working alone in a room.

"When we first became writing partners, we were just working as assistants and barely getting by," Dworkin said. "We got along well when we met during one of those assistant gigs, and it made sense to team up. We wrote our first feature while continuing our day jobs. It took nine months, and it didn't sell. But the feedback was encouraging enough that we quit our jobs to write full time. We wrote our second feature in various coffee shops over the next year. We piled up debt, but we didn't care.

"We decided to try writing TV because we thought it would be easier to break in as TV writers. We wrote a *CSI* spec, then a *Practice* episode. That got us an agent to go with our manager. We had some meetings, but no offers, and our new feature was stalling out in the market after a buyer had reneged on a deal (the funeral episode). Then, late in June, we suddenly had action. In one week, we received two offers. A production company bought our feature, and we were offered a free-lance episode of a new TV show. Dick Wolf was doing an update of *Dragnet* for ABC. It was a great week. That was one year ago. And we've been working steadily since."

How did the inner workings of all these various deals play themselves out while they were feverishly writing? "We met with the show runner to talk about our episode. But the new show hadn't been fully conceived. So we did the best we could to come up with a story that would fit in that model."

Meanwhile, their movie was moving forward at the minor studio that purchased it. Days after it sold, the studio's boss left, and a replacement took his place. That could have killed the script, but their representatives told them that this was good for them. Fortunately, when a high profile, Oscar-winning writer came on board as producer, the script looked to be close to a green light. However, time went by quickly and six weeks went by without anyone associated with the purchase of the script making contact.

Back in the *Dragnet* world: "We were determined to impress the show runner. We worked to crank out pages and managed to get three acts done in two days. Then the show runner called and said he was leaving the show. So we stopped writing and waited to see what was going to happen. The new show runner was very cool. We thought we'd have to trash all our work and start over, but he had us finish the draft. It was good enough that he offered us a staff position and the security of working on a network show."

Unfortunately, in Hollywood, there's a disappointment and a frustration for every exciting success. Ten weeks after the sale, the pair had yet to meet with anyone about the rewrite. But they were summoned to a table read of *Dragnet* at the Four Seasons with the actors. Now, why should a network hour drama do a table read at the office when it can head to a five-star hotel and enjoy a gourmet buffet while reading the script? Fortunately, the food was good — which helped numb the pain of more cancelled meetings and a total lack of action for three months on the pair's movie.

"At *Dragnet*, the lead actor was fired, and Ed O'Neill was brought in. Our episode was first up for preproduction. We found ourselves involved in casting, art direction, wardrobe, et cetera. We were consulted and invited into the process more than anything we expected. It was all gratifying and unexpected. When we shot our first episode, we were on the set, watching the script come to life."

The movie war continued, and five months after the sale, the pair had their meeting — but not with the Oscar-winning writer. His development staff showed up instead. "They had generated some ideas for the rewrite. From a logic standpoint, their core idea was flawed, but they didn't want to hear it. We held out hope we could retain the integrity of our story.

"A month later we all gathered at a friend's house to watch our first broadcast with our names on-screen for the first time. Our mothers were proud. We wrote a second and third episode. We were eventually credited with four of the twelve episodes that aired. Then it was a question of whether or not the show would get picked up for the following season. We were right on the bubble. It was a nerve-racking yet stimulating facet of the medium. ABC picked up the show for thirteen more episodes. We got a promotion and a raise." (Unfortunately, the show ended during its second season before publication.)

But whatever happened to that movie of theirs? "After generating thirty pages of new material, we were told to do the studio's notes point for point. It was tough, but we made it work. Executing the notes was difficult and frustrating, but the draft was okay. We again felt optimistic. There was hope for this project yet. We turned it in and looked forward to hearing the thoughts of the Oscar-winning writer/producer. We were assured he would read the script promptly. It would be nice to finally talk to him. But, a year after the sale, evolution stalled. We have yet to speak to our Oscar-winning writer/producer. We have no idea what he thought of the script. We put an enormous amount of energy into this project. We expect the project to go into turnaround shortly."

The pair is writing a new feature now — a horror movie. The goal is to write a script immune to studio notes — if that's even possible.

"TV is rewarding, and we enjoy it. We hope to have a career in the medium for years to come, but film is our first love. It's going to take a lot more than one disheartening development experience to temper our desire to make movies."

THE AFTERLIFE
What a writer's heaven and hell might be like.

chapter ten

The Reality Show:
Who Says There's No Work Out There?

The reality TV phenomena hit TV so hard and so fast that this chapter was not included in my original outline for this book. Sure, there were always primetime reality shows on TV since the dawn of the medium — including *Candid Camera*, *Real People*, and any number of game shows. But the current crop of shows is so voracious that it's eating up a lot of primetime hours. No book on writing for film and TV industry would be complete without considering reality TV's powerful and potentially long-lasting effects.

There's a common gripe among writers in the TV writing business that reality shows (or unscripted television) are killing the job market. With so many networks and cable outlets filling their weekly lineups with *Survivor*, *Joe Millionaire*, *Queer Eye for the Straight Guy*, and their kin, scriptwriters who came up looking to write one-hour-dramas or sitcoms suddenly feel as through there's no place for them. If that's the case, why am I constantly meeting writers who work for these reality shows? Is it possible that the term "unscripted" is somehow a misnomer? Are those out-of-work writers still looking for jobs because reality shows killed the TV market? On the other hand, are they just unwilling to open their minds and "lower" themselves to working in unscripted television? I think it's the latter, so it should help to learn more about this genre.

Shari Brooks

Shari Brooks, story editor on the popular and groundbreaking reality show *The Osbornes*, worked in both scripted and unscripted TV and admits the transition between the genres is difficult, but hardly impossible. While in the USC Master of Professional Writing Program, Brooks interned at MTV's *The Real World*. She was then hired after graduation as the show's night transcriber, putting in long hours logging the day's footage. After a few weeks of that hard duty, she transitioned to a day job as assistant story editor.

"I eventually story-edited some episodes during the season," Brooks said. "But I really wanted to work in comedy."

Brooks left *The Real World* to find employment in sitcoms as a writer's assistant. But how did she manage to get one of the highly coveted writer's assistant gigs? "It's really difficult to get a writer's assistant job — even to get one as an unpaid internship. But once you have your first job and you've proven yourself, you'll be recommended and will move from show to show. The trick can be not being too good at it because you could end up getting pigeon-holed as a writing assistant."

Brooks recommended pouring through the *Hollywood Reporter* for shows that are picked up as pilots. Get the line producer's name and fax number from the shows and cover the city with resumés.

"For my first show, I sent a resumé to every show in town and got multiple interviews and multiple job offers. You have to be willing to take any job. Some people start as a PA."

As an assistant, she worked on six different sitcoms over a few years. That eventually led to work as a script coordinator — offering her the chance to pitch jokes and stories occasionally to producers.

"I co-wrote an episode of *Caroline in the City*. Switching over was difficult because it's not easy making transactions as a writer. People are generally cautious over writers looking to transition. It's easier to pigeonhole someone rather than allow him or her to write both comedy and drama or comedy and unscripted."

Brooks then found herself back at MTV. While there, she learned that *The Osbornes* producers were doing a pilot for that show. She got aboard and has been there for all three seasons. "I worked on other shows at MTV," she added.

But what does a writer do in a medium that is supposed to feature naturally occurring, nonfiction narratives? After all, is there any room for a writer to create a story in unscripted show? There is because what a scriptwriter does on any reality show is the same as what any writer does all the time — search for the stories that arise in everyday life.

"It's possible to put a show together if you know basic storytelling. You cull the show from a huge amount of footage. *Real World* helped to train me for the story editor job here on *The Osbornes* because I learned how to find, track, and develop the stories already present in the footage."

"A sitcom writer sits in a room with a bunch of people pitching stories and jokes. But a reality show writer is sitting alone in a room watching hours of tape and pulling a story together from all of it."

Brooks and company at *The Osbornes* has about three weeks to put one episode together. For the episode that she was working on at the time, she watched upwards of ninety tapes of 30 to 40 minutes each. That's an average of 3,150 minutes or 52.5 hours of tape she had to absorb in a three-week period. And that doesn't include writing and editing time.

"Working on *The Osbornes* is surreal because — while watching all of this tape — I'm living with these people, even though I've never really met them."

In the future, Brooks would like to sell her own show. She could perhaps produce her own reality show. "I also love the process of putting together sitcoms. And having the audience there on shoot night is an experience you don't get on reality shows. I'd also love someday to go back to long-form screenplays and perhaps write a novel down the road, but that'll have to wait."

Danny Breen
Danny Breen graduated from Belmont-Abbey, a small college best known for beginning the coaching career of basketball legend Al McGuire — the wild coach who led Marquette University to a Final Four championship. Breen's career turned out to be as unpredictable as McGuire's coaching antics.

"I moved to Chicago, hoping to get involved with Second City. I did that for four years, and a lot of my writing skills came out of that experience." From there, Breen got a job writing and performing for the 1980s HBO comedy show, *Not Necessarily the News*. He jumped between a series of pilots, guest shots, and commercials.

"I was working consistently, but I couldn't plan out a year in my career. So, I decided to use my writing skills. I worked on game shows, talk shows, and sketch shows. During that time, I worked with Fred Silverman on a lot of shows. He was a classic — the prototype network executive. He knew what the guy at home wanted to watch, and he helped to make me aware of what television was all about."

In his recent career, Breen worked on *Whose Line Is It Anyway?*, the Emmy-winning *Wayne Brady Show* and *Ellen*. Some of those shows want to give the impression that there are no writers involved with the show. For example, *Whose Line...* prides itself on seeming entirely like an improv show. But bits have to be invented — and situations have to be conceived to put into skits. Also, whatever monologues the host might use and any humorous desk bits must be written.

Breen explained, "Whether you're writing sitcoms or selling screenplays, as with any writing, most writers are in for a rude awakening. Very rarely do you get to write your own vision. You figure out what they want and write to it. That's how you keep writing. Fortunately, in my current job, Ellen DeGeneres is really very talented. She's easy to write for because you know work will be in good hands. She has an amazing gift of taking what you write and making it her own. All the writers were able to write what they want. In the office, we all spent the first couple of months writing material and piling monologue ideas, desk pieces and sketches for the show."

On show days at *Ellen*, the production tapes daily at 5:30. When writing for that day's show, the producers are on the writers to be doing something specific. "Once we're on the air, we can move to topical things going on and come up with ideas for the next day's show. If your show is airing in daytime, like ours, you're probably going to stick to pop culture material. And there's always a lot of research with TV writing. You have people who rely on that research to determine what audience tunes in to watch — what audience you have to write for as a writer. We're given a demographic of what the audience is, and they usually shoot low. Ironically, at Second City, we had to approach the material as if the audience was as intelligent as we were, or more so. And I think that that's a good way to approach material. Unfortunately, that's not the case in television."

How does one break into reality show writing? As with sitcoms, Breen said the reality show producers want to hire younger people who don't have a life yet. "They're going to take that life away. The people who last and make it through that move up to be show runners. Then you can put something on the air that's your sensibility."

Another way to break into unscripted television is to find one of the growing number of agents who represent such writers. We'll take a few pages and meet one now.

Beth Bohn

With the tidal wave of Reality Television washing over primetime schedules during the last two years, many TV writers fear a famine. With fewer network and cable TV scheduling hours requiring traditional writers to invent plotlines, will an already competitive field become even sparser and cutthroat? According to Beth Bohn, veteran television agent at big house agency APA, there's no need to worry.

Whether a TV show falls under the reality or "scripted" umbrella, such entertainment products still need to conceive and tell a story.

"You need to have a story arc in all of them," Bohn said. "Good reality shows have a story arc, too."

Bohn added that while reality TV on American networks seemed to come out of nowhere as a phenomenon with the premiere of *Survivor*, the genre existed for years with shows like *COPS* airing for more than a decade. In addition, game shows have existed on primetime since the dawn of the medium.

"It's two different worlds," Bohn said of reality and scripted television. "It's not one new form of entertainment emerging over another. You have sitcom writers as opposed to one-hour drama writers, drama people opposed to reality people. It's all different since the genres have separate hierarchies and individual needs."

Bohn is uniquely qualified to comment on the overall relationship of the different entertainment models as she's an agent dealing in both worlds. "A lot of people know me through scripted entertainment, but I handle both. Different types of people do different types of work between reality and scripted. People that come up with reality ideas are more feature-oriented — more conceptually based. They think in terms of a device or vehicle to get their views and intentions across, whereas I find the TV comedy or drama writers are more driven by individual story concepts."

A native of America's Dairyland like yours truly, APA's Beth Bohn earned a degree in nursing from the University of Wisconsin. After deciding nursing was not the career for her, she went into sales and marketing. "I was always searching for something that I was passionate about, and it wasn't that job. So I went to a seminar that dealt with how to find a career that you love. I loved watching TV and really wanted to watch TV as part of my job. I also loved doing sales and deals on the telephone. From there, I determined becoming an agent would be something to look at further. In the early nineties, I negotiated out of my corporate job and started temping in the entertainment industry. I temped at The Agency in the casting and literary divisions. I decided I preferred literary and moved to the Irv Schechter Agency as an assistant."

From there, Bohn's path took her to The Turtle Agency, The Paul Kohner Agency and eventually to the budding Big House firm, APA. Now she represents television writers, directors, and producers for one-hour series, sitcoms, and reality-based shows.

"I think one of the most important thing for any agent is to be able to juggle their duties. There are so many demands on an agent from his or her clients and the firm's management. A successful agent can push all the distractions aside and really focus on who they need to call, submit to, and what priorities they need to be on top of that particular day. My days can really vary, depending on the season and what the follow-up needs. The important things to remember are whom I already submitted to, whom I should follow up on, and whom I need to call and introduce clients to around town. Also, an agent needs to make sure that they are totally focused when the time comes to negotiate the deals."

Surprisingly, Bohn said there isn't a significant difference in business practices as she moves from one-hour drama to sitcom to reality shows:

"The sales principles are the same. It's hearing what the producers (or buyers) need and seeing who you have that fits that need. In the reality TV world, it's a smaller community. Most started out as runners or PAs for Dick Clark or Merv Griffin. They all know each other. With primetime half-hours, they obviously look for people who are funny and can write funny material. In one-hour dramas, they look for someone who can write for the medium because it really depends on what the show needs. Across the whole realm, it comes down to the writers having material that matches the individual show. People that are prepared have more than one sample. I find that when new writers get to their third spec script, that's when the business starts making sense to them with regard to their writing. By the same time, they have pulled together their support group of people that they can trust to read their work and give them good notes. One difficulty that I have when people send me their work is that they're writing their specs hoping to please others. Their voice doesn't come through. When I read something original, it'll be wonderful, creative, and unique. For writers, it's important that their spec script stand out the same way. A spec script has to be outstanding and memorable. When you read it, it has to be different from any of the other specs I've read of that show. When producers read an original spec script, they'll want to meet the writers that have the fresh ideas. They need someone to come up with really creative ideas."

As for ways for writers to work their way into the reality TV world, Bohn explained that the same smart practice still applies — be willing to start at the bottom and work your way up.

"The reality people tend to find work much like the scripted people do. They work their way up from PA through producer to writer or show runner. Many of my reality clients come up through game shows or entry-level jobs for other reality TV shows. That's how it usually works for scripted, too."

In the end, whether an hour of TV is filled with a drama, comedy, game show, or reality product, it gets on the air through hard work — and only hard work earns a writer a shot to contribute to those shows.

section four

Leaving the Room

No.

chapter eleven

Appealing Behavior:
Professional Rituals the Industry Loves

This won't come as a surprise to you, I know, but you are not writing your script for the enjoyment or profit of other writers. Sure, their opinions can be of help in editing or fine-tuning your work, but writers don't buy and sell your scripts. Agents, managers, lawyers, and producers handle that end of the business. To that end, I specifically went out and found such professionals who I trusted to give useful advice. Such input is essential because you do most of your work "alone in a room" and can miss out on some of the trends and recommendations from the pros slugging it out in the script sale trenches every day.

I know the folks offering their advice here, and I can vouch for their exceptional experience and generosity as people. They're good folks who will shake your hand and look you in the eye. But they're also extremely smart, savvy, and tough — tough enough to be successful in the violent world of Hollywood deal making. I wanted them to comment on how you should conduct and present yourself while you're alone working and afterward when you're taking your stories out into the marketplace. What professional practices do producers, agents, managers, and lawyers expect from you? What kind of deportment should you expect from them? By the end of this section, you'll have a better mental picture of how the people in the business end of the industry handle writers — and how you should handle them.

And, I should just get it out of the way and admit that I'm rep'd by Benderspink, so I'm a little biased. For a company that's so successful and influential, these guys are amazingly upbeat, cordial and approachable. Maybe they don't know they're Hollywood big shots yet. So let's get to them before they figure it out.

J. C. Spink

Every era in Hollywood seems to have those representatives who are the absolute kinds of spec-script sales. In the 1990s it was the "Carlson and Gasmer" team at ICM knocking the ball out of the park most often. For a while, it was agent-turned-producer Gavin Palone. These days, the hottest tandem going in the spec world is Chris Bender and J. C. Spink of the powerful management and production entity Benderspink. Now, producer and manager Spink has some encouraging news for the aspiring writers out there. "It's the best one line of advice that I was ever given, and I carry it with me. The only thing that separates you from Scott Rudin is the material. If you can get your hands on a great piece of material, you are going to end up producing that project with success."

Meanwhile, the only things separating J. C. (executive producer for the classic horror/thriller *The Ring* and *The Butterfly Effect*) from that aforementioned Hollywood icon is Spink's humility and approachability. He welcomes queries from serious aspiring professionals and prides himself on being able to spot and develop talent.

Spink's career history is fairly brief and straightforward. He attended Bucknell University in Pennsylvania. Upon graduation, Spink found that there were few Bucknell graduates in Hollywood, but he managed to chase down one supportive alum at New Line. That connection led to an internship at the influential management/production firm, Zide

Entertainment. After the internship, Spink worked his way over to a position as Warren Zide's assistant, serving on that desk for about a year. Not long after, Spink opened up Benderspink with manager producer Chris Bender — also a veteran of Zide Entertainment. Benderspink runs the management and production gamut; selling client scripts to entities across the industry, developing their clients' careers, and producing some client scripts in-house. Spink respects and works for his writing clients because he originally intended to be a writer in Hollywood himself.

"I came out here wanting to be a writer and realized very quickly that I wasn't a good one. After you spend six months writing a spec script, there's a 75% chance that nothing is ever going to happen with it. There's that two-day window when it's sent out and you hope something happens with it. After that, it's another six months to hammer out the next script if nothing happens. It took about a month for me to figure that out. I have a lot of respect for writers out there who can stick with that."

Spink added that it can often be a rude awakening when wannabe screenwriters realize the hard truths of their ambitious careers. "All you hear about out there are your Tarantinos and other overnight success stories. You don't hear about the majority of writers that come out here, fail, and go home in six months."

However, Spink points out that the "how's and why's" of success in Hollywood are never all-or-nothing propositions. There are always alternatives. "I came out here to be in the movie business, and there are many ways into that. I had to realize that writers, directors, and producers all work hand in hand and contribute something to the overall package. When I first came out here, I didn't know what producing was, but if you're out here in the business, you should try different aspects of it to improve your chances of success."

And Spink has definitely made the most of his chances with a sharp eye for talent and good material. "While I didn't have the knack for writing good scripts, I have the ability to identify good material and spot talent. There's not enough great material out there that, if you write a great script, it won't get discovered."

When Spink does discover a diamond in the rough, he enjoys "breaking" the career of the writer responsible. That's not as foreboding as it sounds since it means that aspiring writer finally develops some heat, gets rolling professionally, and enjoys new opportunities.

"That is the most enjoyable part of my career. Sure, the more established people out there bring the opportunity to make more money on the deals, but it's more satisfying to me to get that first deal done for a new writer."

With that in mind, Spink encourages aspiring writers to contact him when they're ready to push their career ahead. He just warns everyone to remain patient, considering his ever-accelerating professional schedule: "When I feel I'm too good to talk to new writers," Spink suggests, "that's when I'll be screwing this up."

When Spink finds that new writer and decides to rep his or her material, he turns to his partner to drive the script through the development process before submissions. "In sports terms, I consider myself the scout, as opposed to a coach. I can recognize good material. But I don't know if I have the chops to edit a script through the note process. Chris is exceptional at that."

Bender works as an on-set producer during the company's motion picture productions. J. C. holds down the fort back at the Benderspink offices, running the show for the busy management firm. Spink also served as executive producer on summer 2001's *Cats and Dogs* with the voices of Tobey Maguire and Alec Baldwin. Spink explained that the role of executive producer is as the professional who brings the many elements of a project together.

"The producer is much more involved," he said. "And Chris is there on set for the films we produce to insure the best possible end-product for our clients' work. We stay very involved with the films here. It's not a case of managers taking advantage of their client's produced films just to get producer's credit."

That's obviously a complaint Spink is sensitive to as the ongoing agent vs. manager wars continue throughout Hollywood. Legend has it that agents generally bear a grudge against managers as only the latter can produce films under California law.

"A lot of people ask what the difference is between agent and manager. Your agent is there looking at everything that is going on in the world of entertainment. A manager tries to make things happen in your career. Managers have relationships with all of the agencies and can send material to all of them. More and more these days, agencies are about packaging. The whole 'only managers can produce' argument is a complaint you hear from the agencies. But there's no difference between a manager's producing fees and an agency's packaging fees."

So, in the end, with a supernatural thriller, a dark time travel tale, and a comedy on their resumé, Spink and his partner seem to have found momentum through a healthy dose of diversity. In fact, Spink credits that diversity as a key element in showbiz success.

"I think anyone who's serious about working in the industry needs to diversify," Spink added. "If I'm a writer, I should be thinking: 'How can I be a producer?' If I'm a director, can I be a writer? The more ways you approach the industry, the greater your opportunity to surround yourself with great material and work on good projects."

Dinah Perez

Aspiring screenwriters closing in on their first option, sale, or writing job often find themselves in a difficult position. They need professional guidance in forging and evaluating a business deal, but they lack the necessary heat to attract an agent or manager to represent them until after that job is done. Unless they have a relative in the business, the best option to seal the deal is an entertainment attorney. Unfortunately, so many new writers are so fixated on the agent and manager solution that they miss this opportunity.

Dinah Perez is a California Bar-registered attorney specializing in entertainment, intellectual property, and copyright. She represents writers, producers, directors, actors, below the line talent, talent agencies, management companies, and record labels. She bills in a variety of ways — hourly rates, expenses, flat fees, and, only occasionally, commissions (only for clients with an established track record). She does not work on a contingency basis. Her average hourly rate comes in at more than $200 per hour. During her legal studies, Perez researched all of the entertainment-related courses. After earning her JD, she opened her own practice and has practiced entertainment law ever since.

Comparing her job to the role of an agent, Perez focused on the specific advantages that attorneys can offer clients, due to their distinct, professional qualifications: "I negotiate deals like agents. Sometimes, I will shop projects around. However, unlike most agents, I can look at an agreement and make sure the language actually reflects the client's desires and what he or she agreed upon originally. Sometimes, a contract can turn on a word. Unlike an agent, I'm trained to look for that kind of language. Also, I will put clients in touch with banks once they have presales on their picture. I will introduce them to sales agents and distributors, which some agents don't do or don't have time to do. If you're at a big agency, they'll help you to package your script because they're getting a big fee and are happy about it. However, at a mid-size or smaller agency, they're not going to do that for a writer or producer. You have to make your own opportunities."

Unlike many industry reps who always charge for their insights and wisdom, Perez shares her experience in published articles. She writes for a website (*www.surfview.com*), and she generates some business from that while educating curious writers on the industry's inner workings.

"I consider educating people on the business and encouraging them to seek a lawyer's advice to be a public service, but it's also self-serving because I got tired of watching people shoot themselves in the foot and coming to me to fix the problem. I get paid three times as much to fix a problem as to do it right, but I didn't want to see writers hurt themselves anymore — especially because, sometimes, writers do things and make deals that can't be fixed."

Perez encourages all writers to meet with a lawyer before they start making submissions. She also believes they should have a lawyer read the submissions they sign before scripts fly out the door.

"If you're writing with someone, you should have a set collaboration agreement before you begin. You need to decide how you want to split up the revenue. Who has the right to sell it? If you don't set details like that, you can find yourself in a position in which you have a script you can't sell because there's an ongoing dispute over the material."

Perez reminded writers that most attorneys offer a free 30-minute consultation: "You can get a lot of insight in that thirty minutes."

If writers don't want to deal with submission forms and their associated risks, Perez will make submissions for them — hopefully easing the nerves of protective producers. "As a lawyer, I take the position that I will make any submission anyone wants me to make. I don't read the material and judge it before I submit it. I don't want to be another obstacle for the material. I charge my hourly rate to make the submission."

However, for Perez, just making a submission is not the main issue. "Writers have to realize that what's important is sending out something that's quality — not sending out something as quickly as they can. I always read scripts that are not ready. I had one client that insisted a script was ready, and then proceeded to send me four additional versions. It's better to wait that six months to get it right, because no one is going to read it again. And writers really need to check their scripts for grammar and spelling. When I read a screenplay that the writer took great care to proofread, I can flow through it. But, when I come across a mistake, I come to a complete halt in the middle of that sentence. There's already so much going against you as a writer, you don't want to give them ammunition. They're looking for a reason to say 'no.' They read so many bad scripts that when they read something that doesn't pull them out of it, it's enjoyable."

Finally, in addition to representing and negotiating for writers, Perez is also an independent producer and is always on the lookout for quality material. For more information on submitting material or on hiring Perez, writers are encouraged to contact Ms. Perez at *entlaw@msn.com*.

Wrapping up this section, I'll let you in on the philosophy of the publisher for this book. They always look for value — ensuring that you, the reader and book buyer, get your money's worth and get the most that you can possibly get out of reading a book. So, in this chapter, you not only gained insight into managers, agents, and lawyers — discovering what they're looking for, why they're looking for it, and what it has to look like when it shows up. But you also just read about two representatives who are willing to read your material and consider representing you. If your scripts are ready, go get them. They asked for it.

The Writer joins a mentoring program.

chapter twelve

Works in Progress:
The Rituals and Breaks of Aspiring Writers

The late Greg Fields, a great comedy writer and one of the best bosses I ever had or could ever hope to have, gave me a great piece of advice a few years ago. He said, "Being a writer is like crossing a river by jumping from one slippery rock to the next." He was telling the truth, but it wasn't exactly the most encouraging news I ever got in the business. Along those same lines, I realize a lot of what's in this book isn't the best of news, either. It was never my intention to write a book in which you were frequently confronted with what you can't do — perhaps just with what you shouldn't do. However, I realize that negativity does sneak into any discussion of the business side of Hollywood. It's almost unavoidable.

To that end, I wanted to fill the last chapter with light — with what can be done, how it's done, and how to do it. I begin with a look at the independent film market and how you might be able to break into that realm aside from the cutthroat studio scene.

The Indie World

Since the early 1980s and the days of first-timer, mega spec script sales like Shane Black's *Lethal Weapon* or Jeb Stuart's *Die Hard*, aspiring screenwriters hoped to write the next big-money studio smash. By coming up with a strong high-concept action film or comedy, new movie writers looked to offer studios potential "tent pole" films —

movies designed for successful summer or holiday releases and capable of generating successful sequels. Silver screen scribbles worked to give the studios what they wanted to jump-start a major movie-writing career. As the independent film world emerged in the 1990s with the dawn of surprise low-budget hits (ranging from *sex, lies & videotape*, *A Midnight Clear*, and *Leaving Las Vegas* to *In the Company of Men*, *Pi*, *Sling Blade*, *Monster's Ball*, *The Opposite of Sex*, and *The Blair Witch Project*), companies like Miramax, October Films, Propaganda, Lion's Gate, and Artisan began offering writers a new market in which to unveil their work.

To learn more about how writers can break into the indie world, we turn to the source of opportunities, independent producers, and directors. They know where the best indie material comes from, how it's developed, and how writers can best market themselves to earn more independent film opportunities.

Rich Hull, an independent film producer, co-produced the youth romantic comedy, *She's All That*. After logging early success a few years ago as a very young producer based in Texas, Hull found himself working with one of the big Hollywood agencies. He hoped that relationship would give him access to the best writers, directors, and materials. He was soon disappointed with the attention and quality of scripts he received from the big house and chose to go it alone as an independent producer. Now Hull keeps an eye out for the best, up-and-coming independent talent.

He repeatedly stresses that one of the best ways for writers to push toward more independent involvement was to continue working on their own material. That way, a writer maintains some control over his or her work and career, rather than relying on low-level development assistants choosing or rejecting their material: "That's the coolest part of the business. You need to keep working on your material and take what the business gives you — even if it's just working on your own spec scripts for now."

According to Hull, developing a portfolio of work for a writer or director is one of the better ways to make certain an aspiring professional is ready to answer when opportunity knocks. Hull raised the ordeal of finding an agent as an example: "The conventional wisdom says a writer must find an agent. Also, to get that agent, you must have a referral. But no agent will sign you based on just a referral. You must have something to show — writing samples, even if they're spec scripts. Agenting is a business of volume, whether you're talking major studio writers or young, independent writers. Agents go where the volume is."

As far as the volume business for writers goes, Hull said the independent film world offers more opportunity for writers, but also increased competition for creators and projects.

"When I started, it was possible to make a smaller independent movie and sell it overseas. Now you need a star to sell a project. The independent landscape is moving back to the old studio star system, and that puts the emphasis back on the packaging of writer, director, and stars."

For a writer to improve his or her chances in the independent film packaging environment, Hull urged writers who do not want to direct to make friends of directors who don't care to write. "Make a friend who's a director. Find a friend with that talent. Work together to get your story on the screen. If you're not willing to get out there and make those kind of connections, if you don't love it, don't do it."

Paige Simpson, the producer behind the Oscar-winning *Leaving Las Vegas*, is a veteran of the independent production wars. She warned writers that they shouldn't come into the indie realm believing it's any easier to break into than the studio system. (Oops!)

"I think breaking in gets harder and harder in the Hollywood mainstream if a writer has written a spec script. It can be nearly impossible to get it to the studios or agents."

As an alternative to the spec rat race, Simpson recommended that writers make contact with companies owned by stars. Most major actors and actresses have their own production companies now to develop material best suited to their talents. "These companies are everywhere, and they need material. They're going to want to compete with agents and managers to get access to the best scripts out there. This is an avenue some writers might want to explore. Also, many investment professionals who once worked Wall Street or managed portfolios are starting their own production companies, as well. They're looking for material and want to get into the indie world because of the digital technology they see on the horizon."

With the success of the video-based *Blair Witch Project*, more filmmakers are looking into the possibilities of cheaper production via digital video. Investment professionals look to develop a library of less expensive product that can be sold in this digital, on-demand age. But how does a writer get to those people? Simpson believes that it's often good to look to your friends or college buddies outside the creative environment.

"The people you meet in the financing world instead of the creative world can often prove more important to your writing career that an agent or prospective producer. You once could make an indie film set in the United States and sell it. But you can't get financing on those sorts of films now unless it'll sell overseas. The independent film as an export product is a reality."

Simpson added that a current glut of independent films has forced established producers to budget $1 million, rather than what once might have been $5 million, to improve chances of a returned investment. If a producer is unwilling or unable to bring a film in for that amount, financiers will find someone who can — without regard to quality. The writer of a good script could end up out of luck. The brightest hope for the independent film market is that many companies are looking to open digital divisions that will focus exclusively on lower budget projects shot, edited, and distributed digitally. Those divisions are willing to finance $150,000 films and could offer writers excellent artistic opportunities to tell smaller, more intimate stories.

Nancy Leiviska, an independent writer, producer and director is currently in preproduction on her first major indie film, *Pub Crawl*. Working closely with writer, producer, and creative partner Stuart Jemesen at Stefanino Productions, Leiviska looks to begin shooting in Australia.

She shared her experiences as she tries to get the script for *Pub Crawl* off the ground. "What we've found about financing an independent film is that it's easier to finance a larger budget film, maybe at $6 million, than it is to put together the money for a smaller movie. The indie world is now making 'more than one film' financing deals. If investors are going to get involved in a film, they are usually more interested in investing more money in more than one film to improve chances on return of their money. So that should mean more opportunities for writers willing to work in the independent world."

She also explained that a writer/director might put together a successful independent film, only to be approached by a studio with a two
or three film deal consequently. But if that director is not prepared
with two or three scripts ready for development, he or she will look
for other projects. That creates a spec market for writers' lower
budget scripts.

"If a writer sticks to screenwriting and does not want to direct, there's
still opportunity in the independent world. Hang out with the independent directors and producers instead of the studio people. To get
to these people, look into what kind of connections you can generate
out of your world. What resources are around you?"

"Also, get on good terms with casting directors who work the indie
scene. They are often mini-filmmakers because they link on-screen
talent with writers and directors to put movies together. They end up
playing the role of casting director, lawyer, agent — a real jack-of-all-
trades situation."

Linda Berger is one such independent casting agent. She casts films in
development, essentially tying actresses and actors to writers, producers, and directors of movies that don't exist yet. In the studio world,
that would be considered packaging. She occasionally earns producer
credit for her work as she provides the elements to make the movie.

"My feeling is one of the most important things an aspiring writer
interested in the independent world can do is align with a producer
because the producer should have access to production money,"
Berger said. "To get a script going, a writer wants to get money. If a
writer doesn't have access to money people, he or she should align

himself or herself with someone who does. You never know what elements will work to make a strong independent film. But everybody wants to make his or her money back. As a casting agent, I can bring in talent to consider a script, but a writer often doesn't get anywhere unless he or she has money or someone with funding interested in the project. I need that to approach talent agents or managers with something behind a project. Everybody in this town has a script. But if a writer allies with money people or people with access to money people, they can improve their chances."

To get those alliances formed, Berger recommends blindly and feverishly networking. Many independent films develop from writers finding private investors, essentially making the writer the producer of his or her own project. She also urges writers to find a good director that might mean something to talent or money people.

"The first question on-screen talent asks when I approach them for a project is, 'Who's directing?' With an A-list director and no money, you can still get A-list talent interested in your script. Otherwise, you must hope the actor wants to do the part because they think it's very well written. It's hard to get anyone great with a first time director unless they fall in love with the character."

In the end, as usual, it's a good news/bad news deal for the up and coming screenwriter. The good news is that the independent market has developed to a level where it can present excellent opportunities to screenwriters unable or unwilling to break into the studio, agency maze.

The bad news is that becoming a successful independent film writer is no easier than emerging as a studio writer. The paths into the separate arenas are different, but the amount of effort needed to make the journey is the same. Independent or big budget, it's never easy. But if you wanted easy, you should have gone into brain surgery or astrophysics.

So, there it is. More less than wonderful news. Still a lot of hard work out there in front of you. Damn. Okay. Let's quit playing around, roll up our sleeves, and get into the hard realities of how you get your script out there. You sat "alone in a room" along enough. Hell — you've read those four words enough. We'll take a direct look at the hard-line strategy of presenting your well-polished stories to the business.

Query Letter Quandary

When I'm not banging out books, I'm a senior staff writer and columnist for *Scr(i)pt Magazine*, the entertainment industry publication. As a regular contributor, I usually manage to say something that pisses off a reader eventually. I don't know what I said on this occasion, but the magazine got an e-mail addressed to me that basically accused me of engaging in fraud. While that might be entirely true on any number of occasions, it wasn't in this case. Allow me to elaborate...

It's fairly simple to sum up the thrust of the aggressive, sardonic, and slightly bitter letter. That string of adjectives sounds like I'm reviewing a fine wine, but in this case, it was a very average "w-h-i-n-e." This reader claimed that that the traditional model of the agent hunt process was a widely embraced lie. As traditionally understood, the routine runs something like this:

- Seek agency representation by submitting query letters.
- Get back responses from the agents you queried requesting your writing samples.
- Send your writing samples.

- The agent reads the samples, has a literary orgasm, and signs you as his or her newest, hottest client.

Of course, I left out a couple steps that frequently intercede in that list — such as "Agent never reads your query letter," "reads it and doesn't reply," or "doesn't like your writing and passes on you." But I assume you can figure out those potential permutations on your own.

Now, the letter that instigated my musings here attacked not only that procedure but the underlying notion held by writers that you could actually get representation that way. The note coughed up something along the lines of, "C'mon. Be honest. Has anyone really ever got an agent this way? How many agents really even bother to read our queries? Aren't we all just wasting our time as writers?" It went on like that, but you get the gist. While I try not to be defensive where work is concerned, I confess my first reaction was, "If so, how is it my fault? Did I create the rules that govern the screenwriting universe? Do I control the wills of agents and managers and command that they not behave as you would like?"

But after that momentary bit of bitching and moaning passed, the first serious reaction was to compliment the letter writer on his bitterness and pessimism. "Atta boy. That's definitely the tack you want to take as an unknown writer confronting the entertainment industry because it's not like the professionals you're likely to meet have to deal with other nasty jackasses all day long. Agents, managers, producers, assistant, development execs, and story editors all lack enough conflict and frustration in their professional lives. They really need just one more desperate, obnoxious person to brighten their day, so please continue publicly bemoaning the unjust world around us at every opportunity."

With that not so subtle touch of sarcasm out of my system, I settled in to do what the letter writer should have done in the first place. Rather than complain about or attack the entertainment industry, deduce a way around the difficult truths and unfair rules and find a way to beat the system. For every unpleasant reality you encounter in the business, there's invariably a constructive way around it — if you're patient and determined enough to find it.

I confess that it is true that the query letter fight at agencies and management firms is an uphill battle. In some cases, they are never read. In most cases, they are read — but never warrant a reply because the script isn't on the reader's shopping list or just because of limited time. Consider how busy the average agent or manager's day is. They have call sheets logging all of the countless phone calls they need to take, make or return. They have correspondence to deal with, either on paper or via e-mail. They have current clients calling in for work, and hot clients that are bringing in enough money to pay the bills. Yes, agents are people, too — and they have to pay mortgages, office rent, car bills, et cetera. So, they tend to follow the money — as you would in their position. All of that fuss and bother chews up a long day faster than an NFL lineman works through a plate of steak and eggs.

For example, when I call my manager, I get a call back — the next day... at about 7 p.m. That's long after banker's hours, but it's an average day for him. If you thought your teacher lived at school when you were a kid, you wouldn't be too far off to imagine an agent or manager living at his or her office. Keep that in mind, and you might understand why you need to write an absolutely earth-shattering query letter even to get somebody's attention — let alone inspire him or her to action. You need to find a better, more reliable way to get to them.

Before examining the end-arounds you can run on the query letter frenzy, it's worth it to mention that there are exceptions to every rule and assumption in the industry. You might on occasion get lucky sending query letters out to get representation. It is possible to catch reps in an open moment — or find a firm looking to expand with additional product. I include some methods that may prove more reliable and a better investment of your limited time and resources.

First of all, if you're just dying to get query letters out there, query producers and development executives. Find companies that make the kind of movie you write, and query them with a one-page letter and SASE. Many of them are looking for material to produce, and you might be making their job easier by allowing them to skip talking to an agent or manager that day. More importantly, if the production company in question likes your script and wants to pursue it, they can find you an agent to help do the deal. The agencies each have separate reps monitoring certain companies as their territory. So, these producers or development execs know the agents well. If there's a certain pro out there that the producer feels comfortable with, they'll recommend you get in touch with them to help get the deal done. And your career takes off beautifully from there.

Regardless of whether that tactic gets it done, you should also always be looking to build referrals. You see that word come up constantly in books listing agents. So many of them insist that they only consider new clients that come to them via referral. Such references can come from their current clients, other agents, producers, executives, or even friends. All a referral does is take the risk off you. Since every one in Hollywood is afraid for their job, afraid to run foul of a psycho, afraid of too much work, afraid of finding a project that's so good they have to invest time and money into it, et cetera. A referral takes the edge off and says, "This person is a pro. He or she has some talent. It's safe for you to consider the work in question."

If you have any friends in the industry at all, at any level, nurture those relationships. They could turn into referrals to agents and managers — making the query question moot. Agents and their ilk want to discover talent because it's their job to find it, develop it, and make money off of it. They don't want to be discovered because that just means there's one more person in the world that wants something from them.

So, in the end, we're back to the question of whether to query or not to query. You can still go that traditional route to find a rep, or you can consider one of the alternative possibilities I mentioned. The bottom line is every situation is different, and every writer has his or her own unique circumstances. Consider what doors are open to you and which you need to kick in before determining what route to pursue.

Indeed, there are as many ways into the big game as there are writers who found them. To fire you up, I wanted simply to include some upbeat tales of how writers made their first spec sale. Every one of the writers I include here was unemployed and unsold in 2003. When this book hits the shelves, they will already be successful working screenwriters. They know too well that, while dedicated writers slave away every day at improving their craft in hope of breaking through the Great Wall of Hollywood, it can often seem like it's impossible for that major break to come along. As the rejection letters roll in and another page one rewrite looms, it is too easy to wonder if it's ever possible to break in. Without question, the best encouragement is real-life tales of victory by writers. They share professional commitment, determination, and persistence, but the paths that brought them to their successes are as different as the movies they helped bring to our cinemas.

Danny McBride:

McBride grew up as a Navy brat, traveling the world with his family. He spent most of his formative years in the tropics — diving and collecting shells to trade for instruments and other musical equipment. I was in a band because I loved music. And that love carried over to movies, too. So, the question was whether I wanted to become Jacques Cousteau or George Lucas."

Once he was old enough, he moved to Los Angeles in hope of making a splash in the movie business.

"I found myself surrounded by morons and drug addicts, so I looked to break into movies. I got a job as a skin prop (extra), and I would watch everyone work on the set — how they would light a scene, how the director interacted with actors, and such. While the other extras stood around and bitched because they were all struggling actors, I learned how movies were made. While I was working as an extra, I met a friend who just got out of stunt school. He talked me into training in stunt work. I wasn't very good at it, but I grew up as a skin diver, and I could free dive more than 100 feet. So that skill kept me working as a stunt man for a while."

During all this time, McBride was spending invaluable time in and around movie sets. He developed an eye for breakdowns and budgets. "During that time, I read a lot of scripts. So I decided to write one. I passed it around when I was finished, and my family or my friends loved it. Of course, that's no real help."

McBride sought professional input from consultant Ann Zald (then of The Screenwriter's Room, now of StoryBay).

"Ann read it, and she was very harsh on the script. But that's what I needed. To make my work better."

McBride's next script was *Zookeepers*, an escapist sci-fi film that helped him cope with the painful death of his grandmother. In that spec, a man is abducted by aliens and lives in an extraterrestrial zoo. That high-concept script got him an agent, and that's when the work of rewriting and working on assignment began. All along, McBride continued writing more spec scripts until his agent hooked him up with the director who would eventually become his partner, Len Wiseman.

"We thought alike, and we could bounce ideas off of each other. We both idolized action movies and directors. We just really hit it off."

That partnership would lead McBride to write the smash-hit action/horror/romance story, *Underworld*.

"I wrote an *Outer Limits* episode, and before I went off to Canada for the production, Len asked me if I wanted to write a werewolf movie. He went to Dimension for a meeting, knowing we wanted to work on a partnership. So we came up with a vampires vs. werewolf concept. I went to work on hammering out this script. Then, 9/11 happened, and it wasn't a good time for anyone, anywhere. That cooled interest for horror and action pieces for a while. Eventually, we started getting bites from the big studios. That was good news because we were living paycheck-to-paycheck and working for that big break with the help of Nick Reed, our agent at ICM. So, we were interested in those studio overtures, but there's no way they'd let us stay on it as writer and director."

The pair decided it'd be best to begin work on another project. They cranked out another concept in three days (an atmospheric thriller entitled *Black Chapter*) and started taking that around town. But fate came calling when *Underworld* sold to Lakeshore Entertainment.

"Three days later, we sold *Black Chapter* to Disney. After all those years of nothing, we had two major deals in three days. So, it was a ten-year overnight success after a lot of nights spent eating Ramen noodles and potato soup. You know how it goes — ten years of watching friends become very successful while we struggled. From there, it was like strapping onto a rocket. Five months later, we're in Budapest shooting *Underworld* with an excellent cast. Along the way, there were a lot of compromises and sacrifices, but it was all a great learning experience. It comes down to passion and a love for the material. Whether you're working with executives to actors, they all thrive on that passion — and they want to see it from you."

I can only agree because this has always been a problem for me. Do I lack passion? No. On the contrary, my drive bordered on the obsessive. However, I tend to hunt my screenwriting goals with cold calculation — saving the passion for the actual writing. Also, in meetings I tend to remain calm and professional — perhaps to restrain my temper in case I detect an open lie or some horrible note. Unfortunately, execs want to see enthusiasm and passion right there in the room during meetings. I pissed a couple meetings down my leg because what I intended as earnest patience and openness was received as apathy. In the end, we writers are considered the artists, and we're supposed to act like them — passionate about our art... and a little off, I suppose.

To fuel his passion McBride recommends watching a lot of different kinds of movies while becoming an expert in particular genres. "I'm writing sci-fi and horror, but I'd like to write a comedy. I might stick a different name on it and set it in a sci-fi or horror environment because people peg you in your genre. Once *Underworld* went, that's all we got for months was offers to write werewolf and vampire movies." But, McBride explained that both he and his partner want to avoid repeating themselves to stay fresh and passionate.

"We keep the spark burning so we still love doing this. When we saw a screening of *Underworld* the other night, the lights came up and we couldn't believe we did that. It was such a hard road completing it. I lost thirty pounds on that movie — and not in a healthy way. Dedicating yourself to a project like this throws your life out of whack because while you're working on it you're in the pit and won't come out until you're finished. While you're working, you must dedicate yourself to that story because people are sick of just the spectacle of movies now. They want a story again. So you have to defend that story through the development process. Absolutely check the studio's notes and take them seriously. They'll fire your ass if you argue too much, so you have to give some things away. But find a compromise. It helps if you just consider the first draft a daydream on paper."

Currently, McBride is rewriting *Black Chapter* and looking forward to the future. Looking back to his marine roots, he compared his career to that of shipwreck hunter Mel Fisher. It took him sixteen years of constant searching to find the wreck of the Atocha — the richest shipwreck in history.

"I feel incredibly fortunate because there are no guarantees in this business — even now. It's surreal. I hate to sound like the boring guy with no controversy, but I'm just so happy to be here, and I'm looking forward to many years of work ahead."

Andy J. Fickman

After graduating from Texas Tech, writer, director, and Lone Star State-native Andy Fickman had the classic "first job in the business" as a tour guide at Universal. From there, he transitioned to the mailroom at Triad before that company was bought by WMA. It didn't take long for Fickman to get on a desk at Triad — booking comics for live gigs.

"During that time, I was still writing and directing. And I started a theatre company. We had some great people come through there, including Anne Heche and Molly Shannon." Maintaining his "day job" career, Fickman worked in development for Gene Wilder and Bette Midler. All along, he kept directing a lot of theatre and writing scripts at night.

"But I didn't show the scripts to anyone. Still, I wanted to move out from behind the scenes and emerge as a writer/director."

Using the connections he fostered while working in development, his first assignment was *Ghost Hunter* for Middle Fork productions. Then he tackled the rewrite and the direction for the feature, *Who's Your Daddy?* To get the movie in shape, Fickman made sure to avoid distractions. "I write more at night than anything. I can do it in the office, or I can do it my house. But I try to make sure I have nothing else coming up. Once I sit down, I don't want to have to get up to go to a meeting or a dinner. The muse tends to strike at odd times. So I want to remain uninterrupted."

Fickman lets a scene "marinate" in his head until he feels fully ready to dive into the writing. And once he begins a scene he makes sure to stay at it until he's finished. He credits some of his success as a writer to his development experience — knowing how the man or woman on the other side of the desk thinks. "Going out on writer's meetings, I'd been the executive. Now I was the writer walking into the room. I had the advantage of working on the other side. I could tell them that and put them at ease."

"It'd break the tension if I said, 'You're not going to hurt my feelings. If it sucks, say it sucks.'"

As an executive, Fickman saw many inexperienced writers damage their chances by handling pitches and notes poorly. "I saw a lot of writers who were green or not all that exposed to that business side. They didn't know when the pitch wasn't going well. They didn't know the clues and cues. They didn't know what was already out there, what the agents were working on, et cetera. There's some added value to knowing the job of the development executive or producer. Most importantly, since screenwriting is a collaborative medium, it helps to know how to work with people."

Fickman urged writers to limit their pitches to ten or fifteen minutes. "When you start to get into long-form pitch mode, using graphics, bringing in actors, you're losing an executive's attention. Executives are smarter than a lot of people think, so don't try to trick them. I've seen a pitch go thirty minutes for act one, and executives don't have that much time to hear a pitch."

Also, Fickman believes writers should stay positive about the executive or producer's project — while also knowing how that new story plays into that professional's past history.

"As an executive, I was always shocked to see writers come in for assignment and say, 'This script sucks, and I can save it.' You're not impressing anyone, and you're not showing any passion or enthusiasm if you think it stinks. So, have fun. Nobody likes a boring writer meeting. But don't go overboard or try too hard. Just have enthusiasm for the project, and know who you're meeting with — what they've done. If they took the time to read your spec, take the time to see their movies."

Fickman added that it's important for a writer to develop a positive, "easy to work with" reputation because no one wants to work with a writer for a year who no one enjoys being around every day.

"I've seen executives find excuses not to meet with a certain writer because they'd rather kill themselves. You don't want to be one of those."

James Cox

James Cox helped to create this the fall of 2003's most controversial release, *Wonderland* — the story of the life and death of porn star John Holmes. The film stars Val Kilmer and Lisa Kudrow. While a student at NYU, Cox made a short film that drew the attention of New Line. The studio hired Cox to writer a project entitled *Highway* that earned a video release. Soon after *Highway* came out, a producer brought *Wonderland* to Cox. Over the next several months he and his writing partners (Captain Mauzner, Todd Samovitz, and D. Loriston Scott) brought a new structure to it.

"I got a hold of a crime scene tape from the murder scene that John was connected to, and I knew what I was about to see," Cox said. "The result was almost banal. I sat there and said, 'So, that's the color of

18-hour-old blood. Bones do shatter like wood. I turned the tape off and put it away. But after a while, the hairs went up on the back of my neck. Something said, 'You have to do this movie.'"

Cox found the story so compelling that he was somewhat mystified as to why it hadn't been told sooner. "The story is continuing to come out, even now. Fortunately, we made the story with the help of the two women in John's life (Dawn Schiller and Sharon Holmes). Over the years, the story found a lot of obstacles and not a lot of truth. But working with real people who were involved with the events, it becomes a matter of trust. There's a level of understanding that's beyond the project. They need to trust you to write their most traumatic memories as close to the truth as possible. So a constant dialogue goes back and forth to develop the project. I like the relationship of working with the truth — working with living people that were involved with history. That interests me more than working in particular genres, so I hope to continue working on projects like this."

So while Cox and his fellows continue working on their projects, you should continue working on yours because, if these four writer can "break in," so can you. There's always room for one more. It might as well be you.

To aid you along in claiming that magic spot for you, I wanted to include one more item before wrapping the chapter. Last year, I wrote a magazine article about a unique service offered by one of Hollywood's biggest stars. I wanted to reprint the piece here — with permission, of course. It's important to share it with you because this unique opportunity never seemed to get the exposure it deserved. It's an online network dedicated exclusively to offering exposure to up-and-coming screenwriters and filmmakers. It's called...

Triggerstreet (Reprinted with permission)

It amazes me every time I hear it. One of this generation's finest actors just opened a pipeline for you to get your scripts to Hollywood... and it's free. With Triggerstreet.com, two-time Oscar winner Kevin Spacey established an online community dedicated to offering aspiring screenwriters and short filmmakers a world to share their life's work. According to the site's creators, Spacey and Dana Brunetti, TriggerStreet is a community of filmmakers and film aficionados gathered together in Cyberspace to share and critique scripts and short films. The hope is that independent and under-financed work will find a wider audience and perhaps even gain the attention of investors or producers.

During an interview from London, where he accepted his new position as director of the legendary Old Vic Theatre, Spacey said the task of bringing TriggerStreet together was a remarkable experience generated by the frustration of not reaching up-and-coming talent: "I found myself cut off from a pipeline of talent that simply could not get material to me. My career was built on first and second time writers. Now, some of the best stuff I've ever read gets tossed over the wall because we cannot accept unsolicited, unrepresented material. Dana had the original concept for Triggerstreet.com, and it's been his baby. I'm involved in the decision-making process, but it's been his drive and intuitiveness that made the site come together."

"It works as a tool for our production company," Brunetti said. "But our hope is for the site to be used by studios and production companies as a resource to find quality material."

"Everyone in the industry has the nightmare of someone sending them unsolicited material and later suing because that writer saw something similar come along. A studio doesn't want to be taken to court. They end up settling rather than going to trial where the case becomes Middle America vs. Hollywood.

Regardless of its quality, if a script is unsolicited or doesn't come through normal channels, it doesn't get read. Everyone talks out of the box. No one really goes for that. So this site is for those without representation."

As a TriggerStreet.com member, you view and review any short film or screenplay on the site. Once you post your initial reviews of other artists' work, you can then post your script or short film (no longer than ten minutes) to the site.

"One of the early problems with the site was 'torpedoes'," Brunetti added. "Some participants were intentionally torpedoing other scripts with bad reviews. That's something we never expected originally when we thought we might have 500 members. Now, we're at more than 70,000. So, if you have a bad review you don't agree with, we'll have a jury room where a group of highly selective members can mediate the dispute. They'll decide if the issue sticks and if the review stays."

Several times a year, TriggerStreet sponsors a Short Film Festival with ten finalists selected from the top-rated short films on the site. Those finalists will be judged by entertainment industry professionals. The site's first festival was judged by Bono, Mike Myers, Annette Bening, Cameron Crowe and Danny Devito. As for screenplays, following a sufficient period for review, if a script is in the top ten, it enters the Triggerstreet.com Hall of Fame. Once in the hall, TriggerStreet will either option it on a first-look basis for 90 days or take it to other companies. TriggerStreet encourages other companies to use the site to find new talent and material.

"If there's something on the site another company wants to produce, we're not going to stop something from getting produced elsewhere."

Obviously, Spacey would be exposed to the prominent screenplays on the site. However, he'll be active as a producer, not necessarily as an actor.

"Kevin isn't sitting there doing HTML code," Brunetti said. "But he was very actively involved doing launch and roll out. He is very active as a producer with TriggerStreet, and whatever comes through the site, he's active in it as a producer." Spacey was also instrumental in making all of these opportunities free to TriggerStreet participants as the site is sponsored entirely by Anheuser-Busch.

"I came into play when it came time to find sponsorship," Spacey said. "Our first meeting was with Budweiser, and Dana and I went in expecting to crash and burn. We'd treat it as a learning experience. Twenty minutes into that meeting, they said yes. It seemed to come together naturally, and only then did I learn that Anheuser-Busch is the largest sponsor of the Tony Awards and the only brewer that advertises during the Oscars. They're also sponsors of AFI. So they got the whole concept and have been very helpful because, while we don't charge, websites do cost money to build and maintain."

Spacey added that he wants the rest of the film industry to take advantage of the site: "It's not just for us. I hope that it will evolve as a resource. It's not just me who can't accept unsolicited material. It's everyone in the industry."

Spacey added that he witnessed TriggerStreet's potential first hand during the site's premiere in Los Angeles: "We were showing some of the short films from the site on monitors during the event. I looked over at one of the screens, and standing there, just quietly watching one of the shorts, were Alan Parker, Sydney Pollock, and Billy Crystal. Now, no matter where he or she was from, that film-maker could never have imagined that moment. I will consider Triggerstreet.com to be phenomenally successful if just one person gets a break through the site — if just one person receives the industry attention they deserve, but could not have achieved, without this opportunity."

An army of one.

conclusion

I just finished reading this book. I read the twelve chapters through — editing, proofreading, and getting the overall feel of everything I wrote. It takes months to put together a book like this, and sometimes what you started with doesn't always fit what you finish with before you type "the end." I really just wanted to see if I felt a sense of unity for the work — if I could encapsulate the message in it to a general statement or philosophy. I think I can do that now.

Screenwriting is a business, not an art form. The subtitle for this book is "The Secrets of Professional Screenwriters," and maybe that previous statement isn't a secret. But you don't hear it stated often enough to those aspiring writers looking to get into the business. It's the veritable 500-lb. gorilla in the middle of the room that no one wants to acknowledge. However, as a writer, you want to be fully aware and know what you're walking into in Hollywood. You want to be the kid who points out that the emperor has no clothes. If you don't prepare yourself for the business emphasis of screenwriting, your emperor will not only remain naked — he'll paint himself bright yellow and do jumping jacks in front of your grandmother. And we can't have that.

When did I personally realize that screenwriting was more about supply and demand than it was about character development and subtext? Strangely enough, the moment involved someone interviewed in this very book. I wrote a script called "Slabtown." It was the one script in my life that I wrote with the resolution of never compromising. I compromise constantly with all of my other work. It's just part of the game. However, this time I had a story in mind, really believed in it, and decided to write it just as I envisioned it — without taking into account marketing trends or industry rules. Of course, "Slabtown" turned out to be the best-written, but least-marketable script on my shelf.

But it did win some awards out there on the contest/festival circuit. That little bit of success drew some attention, and I eventually found myself in the offices of Benderspink, the big-time management firm. I had interviewed J. C. Spink some time before that. At the end of the interview, he asked about my screenplays. I never told him I was also a screenwriter, but he remembered something I wrote a few years prior. (That's a good lesson on how strange events can run in the business. Here was a guy who never met me. But he remembered a script I wrote back in college while he was working as an assistant. Now that he had his own shop, he remembered the script and my name. Talk about a scary memory...). Obviously, I got the script to him, along with "Slabtown."

After a couple weeks, the pros at Benderspink got a hold of me. Trust me — that's really fast for this town because these guys don't screw around. And it helps that they're approachable. Everywhere else, approachable would mean "polite," but in Hollywood, it means "answers their phone and actually talk to human beings rather than making their assistants do it all the time." I sat down with Spink and Mason Novick, another manager at the firm and a former agent at ICM. The meeting went well, and it became clear that they were getting ready to work with me because of the quality of writing in "Slabtown." But, remember that script is a brutal, somber drama. It's strictly an art-house, independent movie in the spirit of *In the*

Bedroom, *Affliction*, or *The Sweet Hereafter*. Still, since this was the script that got their attention, I figured that would be the first story they sent out as my reps as a possible sale or to get me some meetings. Here's how the resulting conversation proceeded:

"We read 'Slabtown.' Good script. Good writing.'"

"Thank you. So, you're going to send it out?"

"No."

I sat there blinking for a few seconds. Maybe this meeting wasn't going so well.

"Why not?"

"Well, what movies would you compare it to?"

I mentioned those same three films — *In the Bedroom*, *Affliction*, or *The Sweet Hereafter*. Spink wrote down each of those and checked them off one by one, explaining, "Didn't make any money... Didn't make any money... Didn't make any money." And, he was right on all three counts. Obviously, this deal was going in a direction I didn't expect and couldn't control. Get used to that idea as a writer. You can't control much in Hollywood beyond what's on the page.

Spink continued, "If we send out this script first, you'll be pigeon-holed right away as the little art-house writer. People will read it. They'll like it. You'll get some meetings. But no one will buy it and no one will hire you because it's not a studio movie."

Damn. He was right — again. The good news at this point was my successful, would-be managers knew the business cold. The bad news was I didn't know yet what I would be writing for them. I admit that, when I entered the Benderspink offices, I was a little nervous. When you look around the walls, they're covered with several movie one-sheets — all of the films that Benderspink had a piece of over the years. There weren't a lot off indie dramas up there — just successful studio movies. Why was I there?

Spink cleared that up fast: "Whatever happened to that 'animals killing people movie' you wrote?"

I was doomed. To the best of my knowledge, I'd never written a movie like that. So, I stared at them — probably for too long. Maybe they thought I was somebody else. They confused my sample scripts with another writer. As soon as the truth was out, security would show me the door. Well, they didn't have security — but they did have a tough little Sheltie who might have chewed on my shoe.

However, even if "Slabtown" wasn't a script they wanted to send out first, Spink and Novick brought me in for a reason. They don't waste their valuable time: "You remember that script with the whales? What did you ever do with that?"

I did write a script about whales — years ago. He'd come across it some time in the past and remembered it. Now he wanted me to update it, rewrite it, and turn that into the first script they'd take out on my behalf.

So, in that brief moment, I had a decision to make. I came into the office expecting them to represent me — the intelligent, skilled, sophisticated drama writer with the killer spec that would open doors for me all over town. Now, I was being asked to become the big-budget action/adventure writer who came up with high-concept, tent-pole movies for the studios. Would I stick to my conception of myself — cling to my principles? Would I allow myself to be marketed, guided and shaped into a commodity that would work in the industry? Would I consider writing for movies art or business? What would I do?

So, you read the book. What do you think I did? I've been writing more high-concept material for a year now very happily. You work for a long time to get the attention of managers and agents. I see no point in ignoring their industry advice once they're on your side. I find writing high-concept material as challenging as writing more personal stories for different reasons. It tests my ability to execute the craft while always keeping the movie-going experience in mind.

"Slabtown" still lives as a script that I send out to smaller companies looking to work in the indie scene. And I'm also developing those stories that might best combine my fondness for drama with studio concepts. You see, I am always thinking in terms of marketability — even when I'm writing "alone in a room." But I had to go through an awkward meeting, an uneasy compromise, and hours of soul-searching to realize that writing for movies and TV always put business ahead of art — every time, all the time. I honestly wouldn't want you or anyone else to go through something like that. You never know what that moment might be — or how you might have to respond. Still, it's a lesson every writer wants to know.

In the end, I hope this book might serve as "that moment" for you. I don't want to overstate my work's potential importance or place in the universe. I'm pretty sure there will still be hunger and disease in the world even after this book hits the stores. But in its small way, maybe it'll help you along and make you that much more ready to handle Hollywood on your terms. It's the old School House Rock rule that "knowledge is power." I think the information collected here educated, informed, and (most importantly) prepared you for the attitude you're going to run into without discouraging you entirely. Rather than run away from Hollywood screaming, go kick it in the teeth — because you know how the game is really played now.

In short, I wish I'd read the insights of all the writers in this book before I started knocking around Hollywood. I wouldn't have had to go through the disappointments, embarrassments, and dues paying. Then again, what fun would that have been?

about the author

John Scott Lewinski writes screenplays, books, interactive games, sketch comedy, and magazine articles out of Los Angeles, CA.

Lewinski started out researching, writing, and producing public affairs programs for WMVS/WMVT – PBS in Milwaukee, WI. After moving to Hollywood, he got his first job as a writer's assistant for Steven E. de Souza (*Die Hard, 48 Hours, Tomb Raider*) and for the Black Entertainment Television comedy series, *Comicview*. He worked his way up to staff writer and wrote several sketches for the Comicview Players.

Lewinski and his script "Slabtown" were featured at the 2003 Cinestory Screenwriting Awards. His feature script, "Darwin's Game," won the 1996 Mel Brenner Award for Risk Taking in Screenwriting and entry into the 1997 First Annual Telluride Independent Film and Video Festival. His next script, "Forced Perspective," won a 1999 Award from the Wisconsin State Film Commission and Screenwriter's Forum for "Best Screenplay Set in the State." That script also qualified as a quarterfinalist for the 1997 Nicholl Fellowship, the 1997 Austin Heart of Film Festival, and the 1998 Empire High-Value Screenwriting Contest. Finally, he was a semifinalist for the Chesterfield Screenwriting Fellowship in 2001, 1998, 1995, and 1994.

As a journalist, he is senior staff writer and columnist for *Scr(i)pt Magazine*. He also covers the entertainment industry for the *USA Times*, *Creative Screenwriting Magazine*, and *Hollywood Scriptwriter*. In the past, Lewinski served as a new media columnist for Earthweb, Writers Club, *Cream Magazine On-Line*, *Inphobia Magazine*, and *Nautilus CD-ROM Magazine*.

A busy author, he ghostwrote the highly anticipated nonfiction sports title, *Mi Equipo — The Saints of Santa Ana*. In addition, his book, *Developers Guide to Computer Game Design*, is available from Wordware Publishing in Texas. His second book, *Screenplaying*, is now for sale at Amazon.com from Random House/Xlibris Publishing. His previous book, *Screenwriter's Guide to Agents & Managers* from Allworth Press, hit shelves in 2002.

A veteran Hollywood story editor, Lewinski served as Creative Executive Story Editor at Trimark Pictures and was closely involved in the development and production of the critically acclaimed *Ernest Hemingway's After the Storm* for USA Networks and *Summer of Miracles* for CBS. He was also a story analyst for Fox Family Channel, Saban Entertainment, The Wallerstein Company, Evolve Entertainment, Val D'Oro Entertainment, and *Scr(i)pt Magazine* Screenplay Analysis Services. He also served as a judge for the $1 million Kingman Screenplay Contest, the Dimension Films 'First Look' Contest, and the Paradigm Agency's Open Door Contest.

Lewinski's interactive writing includes contributions to the multi-million selling CD-ROM games LucasArts' "Star Wars: Demolition," Broderbund's "Riven, The Sequel to Myst," "Command & Conquer II — Tiberian Sun," "Command & Conquer — Red Alert" and "The Journeyman Project 3, Legacy of Time." His feature articles on game writing and interactive industry trends currently appear in *Amazing Stories Magazine* and *Game Developer Magazine*.

Lewinski holds a Master of Fine Arts degree in Screenwriting from Loyola Marymount University in Los Angeles and a Bachelor of Arts in Journalism from Marquette University. He completed his study of English Literature at Exeter College, Oxford University. He is managed by Benderspink, Hollywood, CA.

index

michael wiese productions
www.mwp.com

We are delighted that you have found, and are enjoying, our books.

Since 1981, we've been all about providing filmmakers with the very best information on the craft of filmmaking: from screenwriting to funding, from directing to camera, acting, editing, distribution, and new media.

It is our goal to inspire and empower a generation (or two) of filmmakers and videomakers like yourself. But we want to go beyond providing you with just the basics. We want to shake you, inspire you to reach for your dreams, and go beyond what's been done before. Most films that come out each year waste our time and enslave our imaginations. We want to give you the confidence to create from your authentic center, to bring something from your own experience that will truly inspire others and bring humanity to its full potential — avoiding those urges to manufacture derivative work in order to be accepted.

Movies, television, the Internet, and new media all have incredible power to transform. As you prepare your next project, know that it is in your hands to choose to create something magnificent and enduring for generations to come.

This is not an impossible goal, because you've got a little help. Our authors are some of the most creative mentors in the business, willing to share their hard-earned insights with you. Their books will point you in the right direction but, ultimately, it's up to you to seek that authentic something on which to spend your precious time.

We applaud your efforts and are here to support you. Let us hear from you.

Sincerely,

Michael Wiese
Filmmaker, Publisher

By Richard Krzemien

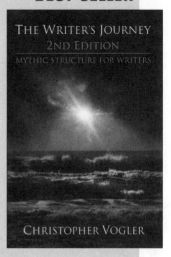

THE ESSENTIAL CRAFT OF FEATURE FILM WRITING
NEILL D. HICKS

SCREENWRITING 101
The Essential Craft
of Feature Film Writing

Neill D. Hicks

Hicks brings the clarity and practical instruction familiar to his students and readers to screenwriters everywhere. In his inimitable and colorful style, he tells the beginning screenwriter how the mechanics of Hollywood storytelling work, and how to use those elements to create a script with blockbuster potential without falling into clichés.

Neill D. Hicks' screenwriting credits include *Rumble in the Bronx* and *First Strike*.

$16.95 | 220 pages | Order # 41RLS | ISBN: 0-941188-72-8

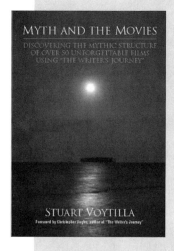

MYTH AND THE MOVIES
DISCOVERING THE MYTHIC STRUCTURE
OF OVER 50 UNFORGETTABLE FILMS
USING "THE WRITER'S JOURNEY"

STUART VOYTILLA
Foreword by Christopher Vogler, author of "The Writer's Journey"

MYTH AND THE MOVIES
Discovering the Mythic
Structure of 50
Unforgettable Films

Stuart Voytilla
Foreword by Christopher Vogler
Author of *The Writer's Journey*

An illuminating companion piece to *The Writer's Journey*, *Myth and the Movies* applies the mythic structure Vogler developed to 50 well-loved U.S. and foreign films. This comprehensive book offers a greater understanding of why some films continue to touch and connect with audiences generation after generation.

Movies discussed include *Die Hard, Singin' in the Rain, Boyz N the Hood, Pulp Fiction, The Searchers, La Strada,* and *The Silence of the Lambs.*

Stuart Voytilla is a writer, script consultant, and teacher of acting and screenwriting and the co-author of *Writing the Comedy Film.*

$26.95 | 300 pages | Order # 39RLS | ISBN: 0-941188-66-3

24 HOURS | 1.800.833.5738 | www.mwp.com

WRITING THE COMEDY FILM
Make 'Em Laugh

Stuart Voytilla and Scott Petri

In *Myth and the Movies*, Stuart Voytilla introduced how mythic structure can help us understand the characteristics of any genre. Now Voytilla and Petri take you deeper into the special world of crafting memorable genre stories. Writing for genre isn't "plug-in-play" formulas and "paint-by-the-numbers" characters but developing an awareness and appreciation of genre conventions and audience expectations. This concise, easy-to-use guidebook — packed with extensive examples from classic film and exercises for developing craft — will help writers of all levels learn the secrets of genre as seen through the powerful lens of myth and archetype.

A writer and literary consultant, Stuart Voytilla also teaches screenwriting and film aesthetics at San Diego State University. Scott Petri is an award-winning humorist who has authored or co-authored 12 screenplays.

$14.95 | 180 pages | Order # 106RLS | ISBN:0-941188-41-8

THE CRIME WRITER'S COMPLETE REFERENCE GUIDE
1001 Tips for Writing the Perfect Crime

Martin Roth

New foreword and updated information by Sgt. Rey Verdugo, Top Criminal Investigator and Technical Consultant for Film & TV

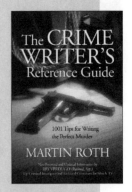

Here's the book no writer of murder mysteries, thrillers, action-adventure, true crime, police procedurals, romantic suspense, and psychological mysteries — whether scripts or novels — can do without. Martin Roth provides all the particulars to make your crime story accurate.

$17.95 | 300 pages | Order # 105RLS | ISBN: 0-941188-49-3

THE SCRIPT-SELLING GAME
A Hollywood Insider's Look at Getting Your Script Sold and Produced

Kathie Fong Yoneda

There are really only two types of people in Hollywood: those who sit around wearing black clothes in smoky coffee shops, complaining they can't get their scripts past the studio gates... and then there are the players. The ones with the hot scripts. The ones crackling with energy. The ones with knowledge.

Players understand that their success in Hollywood is not based on luck or nepotism; it's the result of understanding how Hollywood really works.

The Script-Selling Game brings together over 25 years of experience from an entertainment professional who shows you how to prepare your script, pitch it, meet the moguls, talk the talk, and make the deal. It's a must for both novice and veteran screenwriters.

"Super-concise, systematic, real-world advice on the practical aspects of screenwriting and mastering Hollywood from a professional. This book will save you time, embarrassment, and frustration and will give you an extra edge in taking on the studio system."
> — Christopher Vogler, Author, *The Writer's Journey: Mythic Structure for Writers*, Seminar Leader, former Story Consultant with Fox 2000

Kathie Fong Yoneda is an industry veteran, currently under contract to Paramount TV in their Longform Division, and an independent script consultant whose clientele includes several award-winning writers. Kathie also conducts workshops based on *The Script-Selling Game* in the U.S. and Europe.

$14.95 | 196 pages | Order # 100RLS | ISBN: 0-941188-44-2

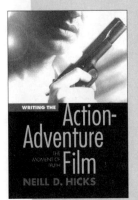

WRITING THE ACTION-ADVENTURE FILM
The Moment of Truth

Neill D. Hicks

The Action-Adventure movie is consistently one of the most popular exports of the American film industry, drawing enormous audiences worldwide across many diverse societies, cultures, and languages.

But there are more than hot pursuits, hot lead, and hot-headed slugfests in a successful Action-Adventure script. With definitive examples from over 100 movies, *Writing the Action-Adventure Film* reveals the screenwriting principles that define the content and the style of this popular film genre. Neill Hicks furnishes a set of tools to build a compelling screenplay that fulfills the expectations of the motion picture audience.

$14.95 | 180 pages | Order # 99RLS | ISBN: 0-941188-39-6

WRITING THE THRILLER FILM
The Terror Within

Neill D. Hicks

A good Thriller will rupture the reality of your everyday world. It will put you on guard. Make you *aware*. That is the disquieting objective — successfully achieved — of this book as well.

Writing the Thriller Film concentrates on the Cosmos of Credibility, those not-so-obvious elements of screenwriting that contribute the essential meaning to a script. To do so, this book traces the thematic commonalities that actually define the genre, and offers corroboration from a number of screenplays, including such classics as *North by Northwest*, *Marathon Man*, and *3 Days of the Condor*.

$14.95 | 168 pages | Order # 101RLS | ISBN: 0-941188-46-9

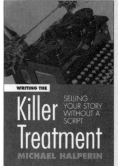

WRITING THE KILLER TREATMENT
Selling Your Story without a Script

Michael Halperin

The most commonly heard phrase in Hollywood is not "Let's do lunch." In reality, the expression you'll most often hear in production, studio, and agency offices is: "Okay, send me a treatment."

A treatment, which may range from one to several dozen pages, is the snapshot of your feature film or TV script. A treatment reveals your story's structure, introduces your characters and hooks, and is often your first and only opportunity to pitch your project.

This is the only book that takes you through the complete process of creating treatments that sell. It includes: developing believable characters and story structure; understanding the distinctions between treatments for screenplays, adaptations, sitcoms, Movies of the Week, episodic television, and soaps; useful exercises that will help you develop your craft as a writer; insightful interviews with Oscar and Emmy winners; tips and query letters for finding an agent and/or a producer; and *What Every Writer Needs to Know*, from the Writers Guild of America, west.

$14.95 | 171 pages | Order # 97RLS | ISBN: 0-941188-40-X

The Writer's Partner

1001 Breakthrough Ideas to Stimulate Your Imagination

Martin Roth

THE WRITER'S PARTNER
1001 Breakthrough Ideas
to Stimulate Your Imagination

Martin Roth

This book is the complete source, as reliable and indispensable as its title implies. Whether you're looking for inspiration for new plotlines and characters or need help fleshing out your characters and settings with depth, detail, color, and texture, Martin Roth will turn your script into a strong, memorable work. This comprehensive classic covers every major genre, from action to suspense to comedy to romance to horror. With *The Writer's Partner*, you'll feel like you're in a roomful of talented writers helping you to perfect your screenplay!

$19.95 | 349 pages | Order # 3RLS | ISBN: 0-941188-32-9

ORDER FORM

MICHAEL WIESE PRODUCTIONS
11288 VENTURA BLVD., # 621
STUDIO CITY, CA 91604
E-MAIL: MWPSALES@MWP.COM
WEB SITE: WWW.MWP.COM

WRITE OR FAX FOR A FREE CATALOG

PLEASE SEND ME THE FOLLOWING BOOKS:

TITLE	ORDER NUMBER (#RLS _____)	AMOUNT
	SHIPPING	
	CALIFORNIA TAX (8.00%)	
	TOTAL ENCLOSED	

PLEASE MAKE CHECK OR MONEY ORDER PAYABLE TO:

MICHAEL WIESE PRODUCTIONS

(CHECK ONE) ____ MASTERCARD ____VISA ____AMEX

CREDIT CARD NUMBER _____

EXPIRATION DATE _____

CARDHOLDER'S NAME _____

CARDHOLDER'S SIGNATURE _____

SHIP TO:

NAME _____

ADDRESS _____

CITY _____ STATE _____ ZIP _____

COUNTRY _____ TELEPHONE _____